Maple
Syrup
COOKBOOK

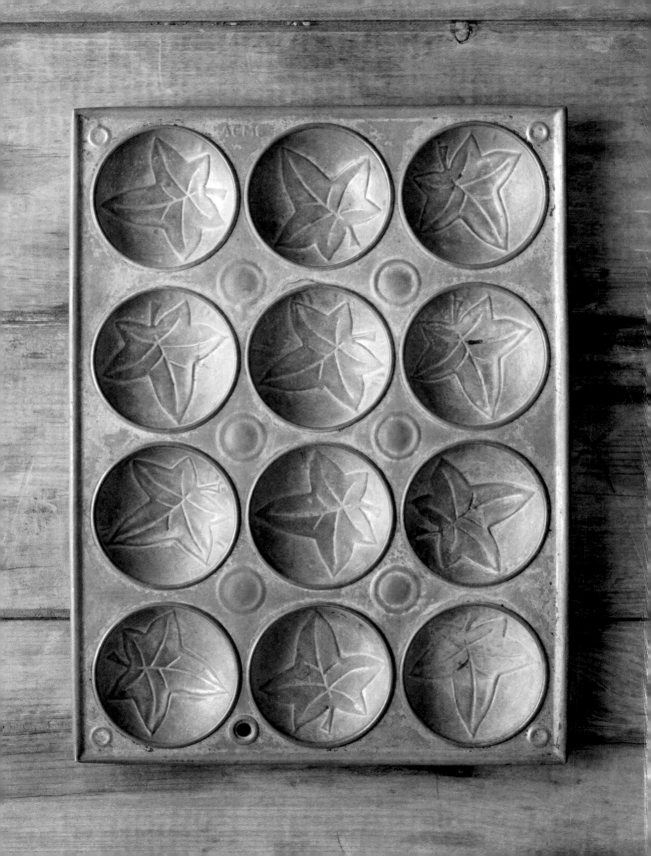

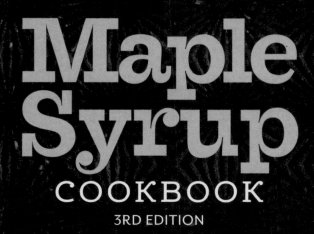

Maple Syrup

COOKBOOK
3RD EDITION

Over 100 Recipes for Breakfast, Lunch & Dinner

KEN HAEDRICH

Photography by
Michael Piazza

Foreword by Marion Cunningham

Storey Publishing

*The mission of Storey Publishing is to serve our customers by
publishing practical information that encourages
personal independence in harmony with the environment.*

Edited by Margaret Sutherland and Sarah Guare
Art direction and cover design by Mary Winkelman Velgos
Production design by Theresa Wiscovitch
Indexed by Christine R. Lindemer, Boston Road Communications

Cover and interior photography by © Michael Piazza Photography, except for © Bev
    Haedrich, back cover (author); © Roderick Chen/Getty Images, 135; © Stephen
    Groleau/Alamy, front cover (top)
Photo styling by Catrine Kelty

Storey Publishing
210 MASS MoCA Way
North Adams, MA 01247
www.storey.com

Printed in China by Toppan Leefung Printing Ltd.
10 9 8 7 6 5 4 3 2 1

LIBRARY OF CONGRESS CATALOGING-IN-PUBLICATION DATA

Haedrich, Ken, 1954– author.
  Maple syrup cookbook / Ken Haedrich ; foreword by Marion Cunningham, author of
    The Fannie Farmer Cookbook. — 3rd edition.
    pages cm
  Includes index.
  ISBN 978-1-61212-664-7 (pbk. : alk. paper)
  ISBN 978-1-61212-665-4 (ebook) 1. Cooking (Maple sugar and syrup) I. Title.
TX767.M3H34 2015
641.6'364—dc23
                                                    2015029141

Dedicated to
the hardworking sugarmakers of North America,
the men and women who work so diligently
to maintain the traditions and goodness of
real maple syrup

Contents

one
Maple from Tree to Table

two
Maple Mornings

Foreword to the 1st Edition

IN THE TRADITIONS of the past, Ken Haedrich and I would be exchanging recipes over the back fence, as good friends and neighbors used to do. And judging from the recipes Ken has gathered here in the Maple Syrup Cookbook, a gratifying exchange it would have been.

Instead of over the back fence, Ken and I have had our kitchen talks over the phone for many years now. And we've exchanged our share of letters. In addition, I've followed his cooking column in Country Journal magazine, as well as the recipes and articles he has published elsewhere. Through it all, I've come to know Ken as a fine American home cook who has great enthusiasm and a respect for simple, wholesome ingredients — an attitude that stands out clearly in his writing and recipes.

Recently, I visited Ken for the first time at his home in the quiet woods of New Hampshire, where he lives with his young family. When I sat down in Ken's kitchen and ate his good warm biscuits and pies — including several of the ones you'll find here — it was just the kind of homey visit with a friend that we all love.

With any luck, I'll be back to visit Ken soon. But in the meantime, if I can't eat his own good maple pies, cakes, cookies, and breakfasts, I can at least keep a copy of this book close by, to make them for myself.

It seems most appropriate that Ken, with his fondness for pure and simple ingredients, should write this maple syrup cookbook. Maple syrup is one of America's most delicious natural foods, and Ken has done a great job of giving us recipes that let the wonderful flavor of maple syrup come through.

— Marion Cunningham
Author of *The Fannie Farmer Cookbook*

Preface

THE BOOK YOU ARE HOLDING in your hands is a far cry from the first 48-page, black-on-white edition of a self-published collection I originally called *The Maple Syrup Baking and Dessert Cookbook.*

The year was 1985. I had been living in New Hampshire for five years, working as the chief cook and bottle washer at a group home for children who'd gotten off to a rough start in life. I loved the work, the pay not so much, so I thought I'd try to make a few extra bucks by self-publishing a book of recipes about a native food product I'd grown quite smitten with during my tenure: pure maple syrup.

Before long, I was loading cases of books into the back of my pickup and, on my days off, I'd schlep them store to store across New England. Times being tight, I would often sleep in my truck, though I can't say that the sight of a groggy, 6-foot 4-inch mountain man in a bulky parka and full beard did much to charm the region's bookstore owners. Or help me sell many books.

In time, the good publisher of this most recent edition would rescue me from my self-publishing misery. And I, a better writer-cook than publisher, would stick to what I knew best: writing cookbooks.

Thirty years and fifteen cookbooks later, I've moved away from New England, but I'm no less smitten than I was when I wrote, in the original edition, that *I love the flavor, the smell, and the color of pure maple syrup, a combination of sensual pleasures nobody has been able to capture with artificial ingredients.*

If anything, I'm even more in awe of maple syrup — and the hardworking farmers who skillfully produce it each spring when freezing nights begin to alternate with warming days — than I ever was. I may not have the need or luxury of using it as freely as I did when I was cooking full-time in New Hampshire, but — lucky for us cooks — the trick to using maple syrup in the kitchen is often less about quantity than it is about compatibility.

More than a few of the recipes in this collection will illustrate my point nicely. Here you'll find plenty of pancakes, waffles, and French toast — favorites where only a generous dousing will do. But you'll also discover how grilled salmon is exquisite served with a lightly mapled mango salsa; how glazed Brussels sprouts take on a whole new flavor dimension with just a spoonful or two of syrup; and how Maple-Onion Marmalade, Spicy Sweet-and-Sour Dressing, Sweet Potato and Bacon Bisque, and dozens more dishes need only a light touch to create maple magic.

In large measure or small, that's what this book is all about: sharing my favorite ways to use genuine maple syrup in the kitchen. It's a journey I look forward to taking with you. Along the way, I'll tempt you with some gorgeous photographs, share my maple cooking tips and maple syrup lore, celebrate syrup-making traditions, and introduce you to the sugarmakers — the farmers — whose dedication to their craft makes it all possible.

Here's hoping that all of the maple recipes in this book, not to mention any of your own adaptations they might inspire, give you and yours as much pleasure as they have me and mine.

— Ken Haedrich

one

Maple from Tree to Table

hough it is widely believed that the Native Americans were experienced sugarmakers long before European settlers arrived in North America, when and how they learned to make maple syrup is a mystery. A Native American legend has it that there was once a time when sap issued from the maple tree in a nearly pure syrup form, something that a formidable god by the name of Ne-naw-Bozhoo decided to bring to a halt. Anticipating, no doubt correctly, that syrup thus had would be too easily taken for granted, he diluted it with water. Sugarmakers have been boiling the water out of sap ever since, in the pursuit of pure maple syrup.

The Native Americans are likely to have converted most of their maple syrup to maple sugar. Liquid storage vessels were few, and maple sugar was far easier to store and transport. They put their "Indian sugar" into specially made birch bark boxes known as *mokuks* and carried containers of it to market. Along with these larger blocks of maple sugar, which they sold or traded, the Native Americans made molded sugar candies. The molds were, as one observer noted, "cut from soft wood and greased before the sirup was put into them so that it could easily be taken out. These molds were in [the] shapes of various animals, also of men, and of the moon and stars, originality being sought."

Colonial Innovations

Early settlers in the Americas brought their innovations to the sugar-making art. Foremost among these innovations were iron and copper kettles, which proved to be far less perishable than the wooden and clay troughs the Native Americans used for boiling sap. Early settlers realized that the Native American way of tapping maples — by cutting deep gashes into the bark — not only wasted sap but also injured the trees. So they took to drilling tapholes with an auger.

The settlers further improved sap collection methods when they replaced the Native Americans' birch bark containers with more reliable ones fashioned from ash or basswood trees. The large trunk sections of these trees were cut to length, halved, and then hollowed out into crude troughs. Over time, these clumsy troughs were replaced by buckets and, finally, by hanging buckets hung by metal spikes. The spikes were superseded by modern taps made to support the weight of the bucket or tubing.

The Native Americans boiled sap by dropping red-hot stones into wooden dugout troughs where the sap was held. And weather permitting, they would also remove water from sap by freezing instead of boiling. The water would rise to the top of the troughs and freeze, leaving unfrozen, concentrated sap below. The large cauldrons brought by the settlers were more efficient for boiling than the wooden troughs. In the kettle method of boiling, a large cauldron was suspended over a blazing fire, supported by a pole frame. Sometimes a series of kettles was used and the sugarmakers ladled the partially evaporated sap from one kettle to the next. In this way, syrup could be made on a continuous basis.

When you stop to consider the laborious nature of sugar making against the rigorous backdrop of pioneer life, you might wonder why the early settlers even made the effort. Were there no alternatives?

Maple Alternatives

There were alternative sweeteners, actually — honey being one. In fact, honeybees had been imported from Italy as early as 1630. But beekeepers were few in the colonies, and honey was relatively rare and would remain so for years to come.

Molasses, on the other hand, was abundant and soon began arriving from West Indian sugar plantations. (Sugar itself, of which molasses is a by-product, was still prohibitively expensive.) But molasses was a thorn in the side of the settlers, not just because of the high cost of transporting it from the coast by packhorse, but also because the molasses trade supported slavery in the most direct way. "Make your own sugar," advised the *Farmer's Almanac* in 1803, "and send not to the Indies for it. Feast not on the toil, pain and misery of the wretched."

Today, of course, maple products account for but a small fraction of the sweeteners used in the United States. However, just a hundred years ago or so — at least in the Northeastern part of the country — maple ranked first among the sweeteners. Whereas a century ago, 90 percent of the maple crop was converted to maple sugar, today only a small amount is, since most consumers buy maple primarily in syrup form for pancakes and waffles. Nonetheless, maple syrup, as more cooks are discovering every year, can indeed play a leading role in the modern kitchen.

Modern Maple Production

In some respects, very little about the process of making maple syrup has changed over time. Today, of course, sugarmakers have at their disposal a number of time-saving and laborsaving innovations, from plastic tubing to reverse-osmosis machines. But these inroads only hasten the transition from sap to syrup; in no way do they diminish maple's magic. The flavor, quality, and wholesome goodness of maple syrup have, if anything, improved over the years. And in an age when so many of our comestibles are nothing more than machine-made synthetics, maple syrup remains an oasis of purity, still made on the farm by men and women whose connection with the earth is part of their daily lives.

Maple syrup is produced in the Northeastern and upper Midwestern parts of the United States and in adjacent sections of Canada, covering a select area from Maine as far south as West Virginia and west to Minnesota. Though the range of *Acer saccarum* and *Acer nigrum*, the two principal sugar maples, extends beyond this area, the unique combination of altitude, soil conditions, and weather patterns necessary for maple syrup production — freezing nights followed by warm, above-freezing days — does not. The Europeans, who have the trees but not the weather patterns, have tried without success to manufacture maple syrup on their own turf.

Maple sap is a clear liquid containing nutrients from the soil and organic substances manufactured by the leaves. It tastes somewhat sweet, with a sugar content averaging 2 to 3 percent, though the percentage can run as high as 6 percent, varying from tree to tree, from sugar bush to sugar bush, from one week to the next and from one year to the next. The sugar in the maple sap is synthesized by the leaves and stored in the tree as starch. This starch is the

"Frog Run"

Folk wisdom has it that when the frogs begin to sing, or spring peepers can be heard at night, spring is imminent. So, many sugarmakers call the last batch of sap that flows a "frog run."

food of the plant, and in fall and spring, with the further action of sunlight, it is converted into sucrose and, in turn, to invert sugar in which the sucrose is broken down into glucose and fructose.

THE SUGAR MOON

Sugaring season begins as early as January and often extends well into April. The Native Americans, for whom this was a season of celebration, referred to this period as "the sugar moon." Sap does not flow in freezing weather, but as the warmer days of late winter return, the sap begins to move with vigor and sugarmakers set out their taps.

Tapholes are usually bored 2 to 2½ inches deep, with a ⁷⁄₁₆-inch bit. A bit and brace are sometimes used, but more common today is the automatic drill. Tapholes are drilled on a slight downward path to facilitate the flow of sap, and they are located anywhere from about 3 to 5 feet off the ground. Not just any sugar maple tree can, or should, be tapped. Those trees, for instance, yielding a sap with a sugar content of 1 percent are not considered economically worthwhile because of their low syrup yields, and therefore are often culled.

Opinions vary, but conventional wisdom maintains that trees selected for tapping should have a minimum diameter of 12 inches, 4½ feet from the ground. As the diameter increases, so may the number of taps, at the rate of one tap for each 10-inch increase. Since tapping subjects the maple tree to stress,

many experienced sugarmakers strongly recommend not exceeding three taps per tree, no matter how large the tree is.

Into every taphole a spout, or spile, is driven. All spouts have a tapered "shoulder" — the part that goes into the tree — in order to form a tight, leak-proof seal with the bark and outer sapwood. Through the spout the sap flows, either into a sap bucket hung directly on the spout or into plastic tubing.

The standard sap bucket today is a 15-quart, galvanized metal container. It has a cover to keep out rain and assorted detritus. Sap buckets are emptied by hand and poured into a central, and usually portable, collection tank. Manual sap collection is a slow, labor-intensive activity, and accounts, according to one source, for as much as one-third of the cost of syrup production.

The advent of plastic tubing has dramatically changed sap collection methods, and most large maple operations have made the switch from buckets to tubing. Tubing is not a perfect solution — squirrels nibble on it, moose trample through it, tree limbs fall on it, and careful cleaning is required. But it has eliminated much of the drudgery associated with manual sap collection. With tubing, one no longer needs to build roads or paths, often through inhospitable terrain, to gather sap. Tubing is light and easy to carry. And it allows for a continuous flow of sap to the sugarhouse or to roadside storage tanks.

BOILING BEGINS

Whether collected by bucket or fed by plastic tubing, all sap eventually finds its way to the sugarhouse to be boiled down to syrup. The typical modern sugarhouse is apt to have one or more large sap storage tanks, a wood-fired or oil-fired evaporator for boiling the sap, a finishing pan for completing the boiling, some type of filtering system, bulk storage barrels for storing the finished syrup, and a storage area for packaged syrup. Depending on the sophistication of the operation, you may also find a reverse-osmosis machine, which removes up to 60 percent of the water content before the sap reaches the evaporator, and a specially equipped kitchen for the manufacture of maple sugar candies.

Maple Syrup: The Real Thing

Maple syrup is syrup made by the evaporation of maple sap or by the solution of maple sugar, and contains not more than approximately 33 to 35 percent water. That, by definition, is the real thing.

Then, of course, there's the imitation maple syrup, sometimes called pancake syrup, that is sold by several national food companies. Imitation maple syrup is mostly corn syrup and perhaps contains 2 or 3 percent of the real thing. For the purposes of this book, when I say *maple syrup* I'm referring to pure, genuine, 100 percent maple syrup. If there is any question in your mind as to whether you are buying real syrup, read the packaging carefully.

Real maple syrup is indeed nothing more than 100 percent boiled sap, but other substances may find their way into the finished product. Generally, these substances are found only in trace amounts and are the result of standard maple syrup production practices. In all likelihood you'll never be aware of their presence. Very rarely have producers been found to intentionally adulterate their maple syrup with corn syrup or other liquid sugars. If you suspect the syrup you've bought has been adulterated, contact the Department of Agriculture in the state where the syrup was purchased.

MAPLE FROM TREE TO TABLE

The backbone of the sugarhouse is the evaporator, essentially a large pan used for boiling water from the sap. Evaporators have come a long way since the wooden troughs used by the Native Americans. The modern evaporator was introduced in about 1900, and its advantages over its flat-bottomed predecessor are significant. Flues beneath the pan not only trap heat and increase fuel efficiency but also provide a greater heating surface, therefore increasing the rate of evaporation.

The typical evaporator is a two-pan affair supported by a heavy metal frame called an arch. From the storage tanks, the sap enters the back or sap pan, the larger of the two pans, where the boiling process begins. Great plumes of steam soon rise from the evaporator as the water is boiled out of the sap. Many evaporators have a hood directly over the sap pan, enclosing a bank of pipes where incoming sap is preheated, which further speeds up the rate of evaporation.

Concentrated sap flows down the back pan and enters by a connecting pipe into the front or syrup pan, located over the firebox. The syrup pan is where the final or nearly final stage of boiling takes place. As it gets closer and closer to finished density, the sap in the syrup pan moves through a series of baffles toward a draw-off valve. The purpose of the baffles is to guard against the constant intermixing of saps of different densities, so syrup can be drawn off on a continuous basis, instead of in one large

batch. The result is higher-grade yields of syrup.

Experienced sugarmakers can tell by sight — judging by the color and the look of the bubbles in the syrup pan — when the syrup is ready to be drawn off. They'll dip a paddle or scoop into the pan, lift it up, and check to see whether the syrup "sheets" or "aprons" off the paddle in the fashion that indicates the syrup point has been reached. The precise tests for doneness, however, are based on readings from precision instruments.

MAPLE FROM TREE TO TABLE

7

Maple Syrup Grading and Use

INTERNATIONAL STANDARD	DESCRIPTION	RECOMMENDED USE
GRADE A GOLDEN COLOR, Delicate Taste	Light and mild, this has what's known in the maple industry as a maple bouquet, or a very delicate but clear maple flavor. It's usually made earlier in the season when the weather is colder and there's less chance of sap fermentation — one of the factors that contribute to dark, lower-grade syrup.	Maple candy, maple cream, cake icings, ice cream, delicate sweets.
GRADE A AMBER COLOR, Rich Taste	The most popular grade of table syrup, this is a bit darker and has a more pronounced maple flavor. Generally, this is made about midseason, after the weather starts to warm.	Used more as a table syrup, as on pancakes, waffles, and French toast, than for cooking and baking.
GRADE A DARK COLOR, Robust Taste	With a deep color and a stronger maple flavor, this is characterized by some as caramel-like and is usually made later in the season, as the days get longer and warmer.	Some find it too assertive to be used as a table syrup, but its bolder flavor works well in baked goods.
GRADE A VERY DARK COLOR, Strong Taste	A very dark, intensely flavored syrup; sometimes called cooking syrup, this is made late in the season.	Some like its very strong maple flavor for a table syrup, but this is most often used for cooking and baking. Its boldness works well with meat glazes, candied yams, baked beans, and desserts that call for robust flavor.

Sap becomes syrup at 7 to 7.1°F/4°C above the boiling point of water. At sea level, water will boil at 212°F/100°C. For every 550-foot increase in elevation, the boiling point drops by 1°F/0.6°C. The correct temperature at which sap becomes syrup, therefore, varies with the location of the sugarhouse and to some degree with barometric pressure, which can also affect the exact boiling point. With late-winter weather conditions in maple country anything but stable — Mark Twain once commented that if you don't like our weather here in New England, just wait a minute — sugarmakers will regularly recheck the boiling point, even within the same day.

While an accurate temperature reading is an important guide to finished syrup, maple syrup produced for sale must be checked for proper density with a hydrometer. At room temperature, the standard density of syrup is 66° Brix, Brix being a scale sugarmakers and others use for measuring the percentage of sugar in liquid. A precise reading is important. Syrup with a density just a little below this level will taste thin and watery; a little above, and the syrup may become crystallized in storage. Because this finishing of syrup to just the right density is such an important step in the making of syrup, many sugarmakers transfer near syrup to a special finishing pan, where this step can be carefully controlled, instead of completing the boiling process in the evaporator.

Once the syrup has been filtered to remove crystallized minerals, it is graded and hot-packed to prevent the growth of mold. Syrup is packaged by liquid measure into standard-size containers, usually made of plastic or metal. The maple syrup, which by now has been reduced from as much as 40 parts of sap, is ready for trading and sale.

Grading and Tasting

Maple syrup grading is based on a syrup's color and flavor. Some of the factors that account for a syrup's grade are the sugar content of the sap, how

quickly and at what point in the season it was collected and boiled, and the rate of evaporation. As a general rule, the lighter syrup grades are produced early in the season, when the weather is colder, and the darker shades develop later in the season.

For more than ten years, an organization known as the International Maple Syrup Institute — a group made up of maple syrup producers, packers, equipment makers, and other industry leaders — has been laying the groundwork for standardizing maple syrup grades across borders. Those standards have already been adopted in a number of maple-producing areas, are pending in others, and — in all likelihood — will be universally accepted within the next few years.

The intent of this initiative has been to eliminate the patchwork of grading systems that have often confused consumers and replace them with a single, unified system featuring color and flavor descriptors to give buyers a better idea of what they're actually getting.

For instance, under the old system of grading, Vermont produced a Fancy Grade, which other states called Grade A Light Amber and in Canada was known as Canada No. 1 Extra Light. Under the new system, the equivalent grade of maple syrup will be known, universally, as Grade A Golden Color, Delicate Taste.

Indeed, under the new guidelines, all 100 percent pure maple syrup available for retail purchase will be labeled Grade A, followed by the appropriate color and taste cues (see the chart on page 8). These new designations are *not* an indication of quality; all Grade A syrups meet the same quality standards. They're simply guideposts to help you identify the maple syrup you like best, no matter where you purchase it.

A second grade of maple syrup — called Processing Grade — is also available and sold primarily as an ingredient in other food products. It is not permitted for retail sale and doesn't meet Grade A requirements. However, it does meet all other quality, safety, and syrup production regulations.

If I were to translate all of this into some practicable buying guidelines or suggestions, I'd say to let common sense and your taste buds be your guide; you can't really know what grade of syrup you like best without sampling them. Personally, I like a more delicately flavored syrup for pancakes and waffles and one with a more robust flavor when I'm cooking with it. You may find a one-size-fits-all syrup that works in your kitchen no matter the application. Or, like me, you might prefer to keep different grades on hand so you have the perfect one to suit the recipe in question.

Finally, if you're in doubt about whether or not you're buying real maple syrup, ask the person you're buying it from. The label and container should clearly indicate that you're buying 100 percent pure maple syrup and not a syrup blend or pancake syrup that contains corn syrup, artificial maple extracts, or other ingredients.

Maple in the Kitchen

I've never encountered storage problems with maple syrup, simply because it's used up very quickly around here. Generally speaking, however, syrup will keep best if it is transferred to clear, glass containers and kept cold. Freezing is the smartest option for long-term storage, one especially worth considering if your refrigerator space is limited. I know one woman who divides her occasional gallon purchase of syrup among four glass quart jars, leaving at least 1 inch of headspace for expansion of the syrup as it freezes, and freezing all but one jar. Then, when her refrigerator supply runs out, she takes another quart out of freezer storage.

While baking syrup stored in glass containers and refrigerated maintains its flavor indefinitely, care must be taken with syrup stored in tin. Tin cans rust, so be careful where in the refrigerator your container is placed. And syrup in a tin package can pick up a tin flavor.

Syrup stored in plastic will usually maintain quality for three to six months. Because plastic breathes, a color and flavor change may result with long-term storage in plastic.

Over time, you may find mold growing on your syrup in the refrigerator. Don't throw it away. Rather, strain it through cheesecloth and then bring the syrup to a boil. Pour it back into a clean container, and your syrup will be perfectly safe to use. Also, if your syrup should crystallize, you can restore it to its liquid state by placing the container in a pan of very hot water; heating melts the crystals.

COOKING WITH MAPLE

Even with these recipes as your guide to maple syrup cooking and baking, sooner or later you may reach a point where you would like to strike out on your own. Perhaps you want to convert a family-favorite cookie recipe or adapt something you find in a new cookbook. How should you proceed?

Well, that all depends. Some recipes are easier to convert than others. A recipe that will end up in liquid form — say, a sauce or beverage — is seldom a problem because the texture isn't likely to be too critical. Some cakes, on the other hand, have a precise balance of liquid to dry ingredients and can be difficult to get just right. Then you also have to factor in that maple syrup not only adds a brownish tinge to whatever it is you're cooking but also tends to make baked goods brown more quickly than sugar does (reducing the oven temperature by 25°F/15°C sometimes compensates for that). Do you want that, and is it appropriate for what you're cooking?

Basically, you have to account for two things when substituting maple syrup for sugar in a recipe: that syrup is sweeter than sugar, and that it adds extra moisture to the recipe. General guidelines for substituting maple syrup are below.

General cooking. Use only three-quarters the amount of maple syrup as sugar in a recipe. For example, if a recipe says to use ¼ cup (4 tablespoons) of sugar, use 3 tablespoons of maple syrup instead.

Baking. For every cup of sugar, substitute ¾ cup to 1½ cups maple syrup, and reduce the dominant liquid in the recipe by 2 to 4 tablespoons. Don't cut back on a liquid that is likely to alter the flavor or texture of a recipe, such as the liqueur, oil, or egg, when you have 2 cups of milk to play with, for example.

You may also need to add ¼ to ½ teaspoon baking soda to reduce maple syrup's slight acidity; this will not be necessary in recipes with buttermilk, sour milk, or sour cream.

If you are serious about getting a recipe just right, measure your ingredients carefully and make notes where you've altered the recipe. Then, using your notes, try the recipe a second time if it doesn't work out as hoped, making the appropriate changes. Read the entire recipe through carefully before you begin, and see how it makes sense to proceed.

And as far as substituting maple syrup for honey, I've found you can almost always succeed with an equivalent substitution.

two

Maple Mornings

tart the day with the glory of pure maple syrup. From traditional pancakes, French toast, and waffles on top of which to pour lots of warm, pure maple syrup, to breakfast breads with maple goodness baked right in, what a way to greet the day. Try fruit favorites, sweet breads, and puddings that make tempting additions to any breakfast table. Make breakfast extra special or wow brunch guests with tasty treats such as potato patties, spreads, and beverages.

Classic Pancakes

THESE PANCAKES ARE LIKE HOME to me. After I've been spinning off all sorts of pancake variations, they're comforting to come back to. They have an honest, grainy flavor; just the right amount of crunch; and a pleasant, cakey texture. Remember that whole-grain flours vary widely in their absorptive capabilities, so the batter may have to be thinned with a little milk to reach the proper consistency.

Ingredients

- 1½ cups whole-wheat flour
- 1 cup cornmeal, preferably stone-ground
- 1 tablespoon baking powder
- ½ teaspoon salt
- 3 eggs
- 1¾ cups milk
- 2 tablespoons molasses
- ¼ cup oil or 4 tablespoons butter, melted
  - Butter for greasing skillet
  - Warm pure maple syrup for drizzling on top

1 Stir together the flour, cornmeal, baking powder, and salt in a large bowl.

2 In a separate bowl, beat the eggs well and blend in the milk and molasses.

3 Make a well in the dry ingredients, then pour in the egg mixture and the oil. Stir just until smooth. Let the batter stand for several minutes before cooking.

4 Heat a large skillet or griddle over medium-high heat, then butter it lightly. Drop the batter by heaping tablespoonfuls and cook until the pancake bottoms are golden and bubbles are popping on the surface, about 1 minute. Turn and cook for 1 minute on the other side. Keep warm (see below).

5 Repeat with the remaining batter. Serve with warm maple syrup (page 23).

Hot Stuff

Pancakes are precious little things, with little mass, so they begin to lose heat quickly once they're off the griddle. And cold pancakes, we all know, hold none of the promise and allure of a hot, steamy stack. Therefore, have warm plates waiting in the oven if at all possible (10 minutes in a 250°F/120°C oven will do the trick). Also, have your pancake eaters assembled nearby, and whisk them to the table as soon as the stacks hit the plates. Finally, have softened butter on the table. I always hate it when I forget this and have to watch somebody hack up a perfect stack, spreading a cold, hard pat of butter on a delicate pancake. It makes me cringe.

Pancake Pointers

For all of their apparent simplicity, the ability to make good pancakes is an acquired skill. Murphy's Law applies, and things do go wrong. This point was brought home to me not long ago when I developed a number of pancake recipes for a food magazine — recipes I had tested to death in my home kitchen — only to hear back from their test kitchen that several of the recipes hadn't worked for them. In the end we worked out the bugs, and in the process I learned that foolproof pancake making hinges on several important, basic principles. Let's look briefly at some of these variables.

The Batter

First and foremost, don't beat it. When you beat batter you develop the gluten, a wheat protein responsible for the formation of elastic strands. Beating toughens your pancakes and keeps them from achieving a light, fluffy texture. So just stir your liquids into the dry ingredients until they're blended. The best tool I've found for this is a simple whisk with widely spaced strands. A wooden spoon or spatula works fine, too.

Even though pancake recipes always give precise measurements for ingredients, it is quite common for the batter to need adjustment. Generally it needs to be thinned, and this is especially true with whole grains, since they absorb moisture gradually as the batter sits. After you've made a pancake recipe a number of times, you will learn the precise consistency and the pancake texture it will yield. Most pancake batters perform best when they are neither so thin that they run all over creation nor so thick that you have to spread them around. I've found that my electric griddle produces better results with a slightly thicker batter, while my skillet works best with a thinner batter.

The Cooking Surface

Basically, the more metal you can put between your heat source and your pancakes, the better. A thick, heavy surface spreads the heat around, and the pancakes cook evenly, whereas a thin pan cooks spottily and you get "hot spots" on your pancakes. Cast iron is superb. I have a special cast-iron pancake skillet that I use only for making pancakes and warming tortillas. It has very low sides, so I can slide the spatula under the pancakes easily.

I really prefer to cook my pancakes on my old Farberware electric griddle, blackened from years of use. The advantage of electric is absolute and even heat control: I just set it at 375°F/190°C and go. Size is the other big plus. I can make six pancakes at a time on my electric griddle; three are about the most I can manage in even the largest skillet.

Cooking

It takes only an initial light rub of oil on your cooking surface to keep pancakes from sticking. After that, the fat in the batter prevents sticking.

Pancakes generally take 1½ to 2 minutes to cook on side one, a little less on side two. When little air holes start to show up on the surface and the very edge takes on a dryish tinge, they're ready to flip. Only flip them once and avoid any inclination to poke, prod, or press on them — that spells disaster for pancakes.

Oatmeal Pancakes

MY GREAT FRIEND Jeanne Lemlin, James Beard Award–winning author of several classics of inspired vegetarian cooking, gave me this recipe. Jeanne makes my kind of pancakes: grainy and nicely textured. You'll want to make these often once you've tried them.

Ingredients

- 1 cup old-fashioned rolled oats
- 1 cup unbleached all-purpose flour
- ½ cup whole-wheat flour
- 2½ teaspoons baking powder
- 1 teaspoon salt
- 2 eggs
- 2 cups milk
- 2 tablespoons firmly packed brown sugar
- 5 tablespoons butter, melted
- Butter for greasing skillet
- Warm pure maple syrup for drizzling on top

1 Whirl the oats in a food processor or blender until they become a fine powder; a few traces of flakes are fine. Pour into a large bowl; then mix in the flours, baking powder, and salt. Set aside.

2 In a medium bowl, beat the eggs lightly, and then whisk in the milk and brown sugar.

3 Make a well in the dry ingredients, pour in the egg mixture, and stir briefly. Add the butter and blend just until no traces of dry are visible. Let the batter stand for several minutes.

4 Heat a large skillet or griddle over medium-high heat, then butter it lightly. Drop the batter by heaping tablespoonfuls and cook until the pancake bottoms are golden and bubbles are popping on the surface, about 1 minute. Turn and cook for 1 minute on the other side. Keep warm (page 14).

5 Repeat with the remaining batter. Serve with warm maple syrup (page 23).

A Well-Seasoned Pan

My special cast-iron pancake skillet has a glossy black seasoning built up from years of use. The seasoning acts as a sort of natural nonstick finish, so I'm careful not to scrub it with anything abrasive. A gentle washing with a mild detergent is enough. After that I dry the skillet briefly over a hot burner, then I rub about ½ teaspoon of oil into the surface with a paper towel.

Banana-Nut Cakes

SOUR CREAM AND MASHED BANANA make these nut-laced pancakes tender as can be. Garnish stacks with additional sliced banana.

Ingredients

- 1 cup unbleached all-purpose flour
- 1 cup whole-wheat flour
- ½ cup chopped walnuts or pecans
- 2½ teaspoons baking powder
- ½ teaspoon baking soda
- ½ teaspoon salt
- 2 eggs
- 1⅓–1½ cups milk
- ¾ cup sour cream
- ¼ cup pure maple syrup
- 4 tablespoons butter, melted
- 1 ripe banana, mashed
- Butter for greasing skillet
- Warm pure maple syrup for drizzling on top

1 Combine the flours, nuts, baking powder, baking soda, and salt in a large bowl. Toss to mix.

2 In a separate bowl, beat the eggs until frothy, then whisk in 1⅓ cups of the milk, the sour cream, maple syrup, butter, and banana. Add additional milk, a tablespoon at a time, to thin the batter, if needed. Make a well in the dry ingredients, then pour in the egg mixture. Stir, just to blend; do not beat. Let the batter stand for several minutes.

3 Heat a large skillet or griddle over medium-high heat, then butter it lightly. Drop the batter by heaping tablespoonfuls and cook until the pancake bottoms are golden and bubbles are popping on the surface, about 1 minute. Turn and cook for 1 minute on the other side. Keep warm (page 14).

4 Repeat with the remaining batter. Serve with warm maple syrup (page 23).

Testing the Pan

When you're cooking pancakes with a burner and skillet, the standard readiness test is to sprinkle a drop of water into the pan. A very active response, sizzling and bouncing, is supposed to signal a sufficiently hot surface. A lukewarm, fizzling response means the pan is not hot enough. This water test is only so reliable, because there's no clear indication when the pan is too hot. You can use the water test to get an idea of where you stand, but expect to do the fine-tuning with your first pancake or two.

Buttermilk Corn Cakes

YIELD: About eighteen 4-inch pancakes

HERE IS A LOVELY buttermilk pancake, one I've been making for many years. It differs from other corn cakes in that the cornmeal is precooked, giving the pancakes a soft and moist, instead of cakey, texture.

Ingredients

- 1 cup cold water
- ½ cup cornmeal, preferably stone-ground
- ⅔ cup buttermilk
- ⅔ cup plus 1–2 tablespoons milk
- ¼ cup blackstrap molasses
- 2 eggs, lightly beaten
- 4 tablespoons butter, melted, or vegetable oil
- 1¼ cups whole-wheat flour
- 1½ teaspoons baking powder
- ½ teaspoon baking soda
- ½ teaspoon salt
- Butter for greasing skillet
- Warm pure maple syrup for drizzling on top

1 Stir together the water and cornmeal in a small saucepan. Bring to a boil, decrease the heat to medium, and cook, stirring constantly, for 2 to 3 minutes, until quite thick. Scrape into a large bowl. Whisk in, one at a time, the buttermilk, ⅔ cup milk, molasses, eggs, and butter.

2 Combine the flour, baking powder, baking soda, and salt in a separate large bowl. Toss to mix. Make a well in the dry ingredients, add the egg mixture, and stir just until blended. Let the batter stand for several minutes, then thin with the remaining tablespoon or two of milk, if needed; the batter should run thickly off the ladle.

3 Heat a large skillet or griddle over medium-high heat, then butter it lightly. Drop the batter by heaping tablespoonfuls and cook until the bottoms are golden and bubbles are popping on the surface, about 1 minute. Turn and cook for 1 minute on the other side. Keep warm (page 14).

4 Repeat with the remaining batter. Serve with warm maple syrup (page 23).

Citadelle Maple Syrup Producers' Cooperative

THOUGH MANY PEOPLE the world over still think "Vermont" when they hear the words *maple syrup*, Quebec is by far the largest producer in the world.

The Citadelle Maple Syrup Producers' Cooperative began in 1925, when 102 syrup producers united to cope with a monopoly of buyers whose low prices threatened to destroy the maple syrup market. Today, according to Richard Acheson of the cooperative, grandchildren of the founders are among the 2,000 producers in Quebec who are cooperative members.

The cooperative's members store the syrup they produce during the short maple season in specially designed vats, from which syrup is tested, refiltered, bottled, and shipped. In the U.S. market, Citadelle syrup is sold under the brand name Camp Maple Syrup.

Citadelle also works to promote 100 percent pure maple syrup by distributing recipes that show people how to use maple syrup for more than just pancakes. And, as part of its maple marketing program, in 1999 the cooperative opened a shop called Canadian Maple Delights in Vancouver, British Columbia. The combination gift shop–bistro features maple products for all occasions and light meals utilizing maple syrup as a prime ingredient. Since then, the cooperative has opened three more bistros in Montreal, Quebec City, and Dorval. Visit them at their website (see page 172 for contact information). (Recipes from Citadelle members are on pages 20, 65, 69, 112, 162, and 168.)

Maple French Toast

IN THIS VARIATION on the classic French toast, maple syrup is added to the batter to infuse the bread with sweetness. A member of the Citadelle Maple Syrup Producers' Cooperative of Quebec, Canada, created this recipe.

Ingredients

- 2 eggs
- ⅔ cup milk
- ⅓ cup pure maple syrup
- 2 tablespoons cream
- ¼ teaspoon salt
  Pinch of ground nutmeg
- 8 slices bread, crusts trimmed
  Butter for greasing skillet
  Warm pure maple syrup, fruit preserves, or lemon juice and confectioners' sugar for topping

1 Beat the eggs in a large shallow bowl until light. Whisk in the milk, maple syrup, cream, salt, and nutmeg.

2 Dip slices of bread into the egg mixture, one at a time, turning to coat both sides.

3 Heat a large skillet or griddle over medium heat, then butter it lightly. Cook the bread until golden brown, 2 to 3 minutes per side. Keep warm (page 14).

4 Repeat with the remaining bread and batter. Serve with warm maple syrup (page 23).

Whole-Wheat Corn Waffles

THESE WHOLESOME WAFFLES have a wonderful crunch and a deep, grainy flavor. They're great with a little plain yogurt on the side.

Ingredients

Butter for greasing waffle iron
1½ cups whole-wheat flour
½ cup cornmeal, preferably stone-ground
2 tablespoons sugar
4 teaspoons baking powder
¾ teaspoon salt
2 eggs
2⅓ cups milk
½ cup (1 stick) butter, melted, or part butter and part vegetable oil
Warm pure maple syrup for drizzling on top
Plain yogurt for topping, optional

1 Preheat a waffle iron and butter it lightly.

2 Combine the flour, cornmeal, sugar, baking powder, and salt in a large bowl. Toss to mix.

3 In a separate bowl, beat the eggs lightly. Whisk in the milk and butter. Make a well in the dry ingredients, then pour in the egg mixture. Whisk briefly, just until blended. Let the batter stand for several minutes.

4 Cook the batter in the prepared waffle iron until crisp and golden, about 2 minutes. Keep warm (page 14 and Waffle Thoughts, below).

5 Repeat with the remaining batter. Serve with warm maple syrup (page 23) and yogurt, if desired.

Waffle Thoughts

There are certain things I like more about waffles than pancakes, the main thing being that they aren't so fussy. You can make up a batch of waffles and hold them in the oven on a wire rack for a reasonable amount of time — up to 15 minutes, say, at about 250°F — without having them turn to rubber like pancakes will. Waffles even taste great at room temperature, or slightly warm; pancakes don't. Therefore, leftover waffles are never a problem. You can even pop them in the toaster the next day to warm them up, and they'll regain at least some of their crispness. They're not quite the same as fresh, but you could do much worse.

Syrup Warmer

If you want your syrup to go further on pancakes and waffles, and you don't want your food to get cold, warm up the syrup first, so it thins out. Warm syrup won't rob heat from your pancakes the way cold syrup will. You can heat your syrup in a saucepan over low heat (don't let it come to a boil) and spoon it out; keep a small amount in a table dispenser and warm that in a pan of hot water; or heat ½ cup of syrup in the microwave on high for 30 to 60 seconds. I'm all in favor of those spring-loaded glass dispensers you see in diners. Since the spring holds the top shut, there's no chance of accidentally spilling the valuable contents all over the table. This is especially useful if you have young kids. When our three were young, our breakfast table was a regular reach-a-rama. Stuff flew everywhere.

Death by Chocolate Waffles

TRY THESE CRISP, double-chocolate waffles with a small mountain of vanilla ice cream and a pool of maple syrup. Maybe they're not life threatening, but they're surely diet threatening! They're the ultimate in chocolate decadence.

Ingredients

Butter for greasing waffle iron
- 1⅓ cups unbleached all-purpose flour
- ⅓ cup whole-wheat flour
- ¼ cup unsweetened cocoa powder
- 1 tablespoon baking powder
- 1 teaspoon ground cinnamon
- ½ teaspoon salt
- ½ cup (1 stick) butter
- 3 ounces semisweet chocolate
- 2 tablespoons sugar
- 2¼ cups milk
- 2 eggs, beaten until frothy

Warm pure maple syrup for drizzling on top

1 Preheat a waffle iron and butter it lightly. Combine the flours, cocoa powder, baking powder, cinnamon, and salt in a large bowl. Toss to mix. Set aside.

2 Combine the butter, chocolate, and sugar in a medium saucepan and melt over very low heat. Whisk to smooth, remove from the heat, then whisk in the milk and eggs.

3 Make a well in the dry ingredients, pour in the chocolate mixture, and blend, just until everything is combined; watch for dry clumps. Let the batter stand for several minutes; it will thicken slightly.

4 Cook the batter in the prepared waffle iron until crisp and golden, about 2 minutes. Keep warm (pages 14 and 22).

5 Repeat with the remaining batter. Serve with warm maple syrup (page 23).

Maple Bran Muffins

WITH THESE TASTY MORSELS,
Joan Lukes of Merrill, Wisconsin, took
first place in the 1999 recipe contest
sponsored by the Wisconsin Maple
Syrup Producer's Association.

Ingredients

    1   cup unbleached all-purpose flour
    1   teaspoon baking soda
    1   cup bran flakes
    ½   cup chopped walnuts, optional
    ⅓   cup raisins
    1   cup pure maple syrup
    1   cup sour cream
    2   eggs

Topping

    3   tablespoons unbleached all-purpose flour
    2   tablespoons firmly packed brown sugar
    1   tablespoon butter

1 Preheat the oven to 400°F/200°C. Grease a 12-cup muffin tin and set aside.

2 Sift the flour and baking soda into a medium bowl. Add the bran flakes, walnuts, if desired, and raisins.

3 Combine the maple syrup, sour cream, and eggs in a small bowl; add to the dry ingredients and stir until just blended. Fill the muffin cups three-quarters full with the mixture.

4 TO MAKE THE TOPPING: Combine the flour and sugar in a small bowl. Cut in the butter until the mixture is crumbly. Sprinkle the topping on the batter.

5 Bake for 15 to 20 minutes, until the muffins are golden brown.

Breakfast Classics

Maple Sticky Buns

IF YOU LIKE STICKY BUNS but can seldom find the time to make the real thing, these are for you. I've taken an ordinary biscuit recipe and turned it into something quite extraordinary with the help of a maple glaze. And I seal the deal with a brown sugar, walnut, and cinnamon filling. You'll want to make these for a special Sunday breakfast.

Ingredients

½ cup finely chopped walnuts
¼ cup firmly packed brown sugar
½ teaspoon ground cinnamon
½ cup pure maple syrup
½ cup (1 stick) plus 1 tablespoon cold butter
2¼ cups unbleached all-purpose flour
1 tablespoon baking powder
¾ teaspoon salt
1 cup milk

1 Preheat the oven to 400°F/200°C. Mix together the walnuts, brown sugar, and cinnamon in a small bowl. Set aside.

2 In a small saucepan, bring the maple syrup and 4 tablespoons of the butter to a boil over medium heat. Boil for 30 seconds, then scrape into a 9-inch square baking pan or a 10-inch deep-dish pie plate. Set aside.

3 Combine the flour, baking powder, and salt in a large bowl. Toss to mix. Cut 4 tablespoons of the butter into ½-inch pieces, add to the flour mixture, and cut it in until the butter is roughly the size of split peas. Make a well in the mixture and add the milk. Stir gently, just until the mixture forms a damp, cohesive mass. If the dough seems a bit wet, work in a tad more flour with the back of a wooden spoon. Melt the remaining 1 tablespoon butter in a small saucepan.

4 Turn the dough onto a lightly floured surface and knead gently five or six times. Using a rolling pin, roll the dough into the best 9- by 12-inch rectangle you can manage; don't worry if it isn't perfect. Brush the surface with the melted butter.

5 Cover the dough evenly with the brown sugar mixture, patting it gently with your hands. Starting at the 9-inch edge, roll up the dough like a carpet, pinching at the seam to seal. Cut into nine 1-inch slices and lay them flat in the baking pan with the syrup. Bake for 25 minutes. Remove from the oven and invert onto a large plate; do this quickly but carefully, being aware that the syrup is very hot. Oven mitts are a good precaution. Scrape any syrupy stuff from the pan and spread over the buns.

Granola

EVERY CHRISTMAS I like to prepare large batches of this granola for my friends and family; it makes a great stocking stuffer. Instead of all oats, you can also use other grain flakes. A portion of the seeds may be replaced with bran or untoasted wheat germ.

Ingredients

- 4 cups old-fashioned rolled oats
- 1 cup coarsely chopped nuts (cashews, pecans, or almonds)
- 1 cup raw (unroasted) sunflower seeds
- ½ cup sesame seeds
- ½ cup unsweetened shredded coconut (available in health food stores)
- ½ teaspoon salt
- 6 tablespoons pure maple syrup
- 6 tablespoons light-tasting vegetable oil, such as sunflower oil
- 1 cup chopped raisins or dried dates

1 Preheat the oven to 300°F/150°C. Toss the oats, nuts, sunflower seeds, sesame seeds, coconut, and salt to mix in a large bowl.

2 Combine the maple syrup and oil in a saucepan; warm over low heat. Pour over the oat mixture. Stir with a wooden spoon, then roll up your sleeves and work the mixture with your hands until everything is moistened.

3 Spread on baking sheets, no more than about ½ inch thick, and bake for 30 to 40 minutes, stirring occasionally, until golden.

4 Let cool thoroughly, then stir in the raisins. Store in jars or plastic bags.

Note: You can use your own preferences to adjust the mix of goodies in your granola. Just be sure that the substitutions and additions add up to approximately the same volume as in the recipe. Some delicious additions are dried mixed tropical fruits, dried cranberries or cherries, and slivered dried apricots; spices such as cinnamon, ginger, or cardamom; and wheat germ.

Hot Cereals

As much as I love granola, nothing beats a bowl of hot cereal laced with real maple syrup or Fruit-Flavored Syrup (page 61) on a cold morning. Besides old-fashioned oats, try one of the following:

Grits. Any coarsely ground grain — such as soy, rye, or buckwheat — can be made into grits, not just the dried corn kernels of hominy grits.

Steel-cut oats. These oat groats are less processed than the old-fashioned or rolled oats commonly found in North American kitchens. They take longer to cook and have a chewy texture, but I love their heartiness. They are also called Scotch oats, Irish oatmeal, and porridge.

Triticale. A hybrid of wheat and rye, this grain has more protein and less gluten than wheat. It has a nutty-sweet flavor.

Maple Cream Scones

THESE SOFT, DELICATE SCONES
are one of the most delicious ways
I know to run up your cholesterol
count. You can imagine how good they
are, since they call for both cream and
butter. Served with coffee, they make
a simple, satisfying breakfast.

Ingredients

- 2 cups unbleached all-purpose flour
- 1 tablespoon baking powder
- ¾ teaspoon salt
- 4 tablespoons cold butter, cut into ¼-inch pieces, plus 2 tablespoons butter, melted
- ¾ cup heavy cream
- ¼ cup plus 2 tablespoons pure maple syrup

1 Preheat the oven to 425°F/220°C. Lightly grease a baking sheet.

2 Combine the flour, baking powder, and salt in a large bowl. Cut the butter pieces into the flour until the mixture resembles coarse crumbs. Make a well in the mixture.

3 Blend the cream and ¼ cup of the maple syrup and pour the mixture into the well. Stir, just until the dough coheres.

4 Lightly flour a work surface; turn the dough onto the surface and knead gently four or five times. Pat or roll to a thickness of about ¾ inch. Cut into 2½- to 3-inch rounds with a biscuit cutter and place on the prepared baking sheet.

5 Stir together the melted butter and remaining 2 tablespoons maple syrup, then brush a little on each scone. Keep the remaining syrup mixture warm. Bake the scones for about 15 minutes, or until golden. Spoon the remaining warm syrup mixture over the scones for serving.

Virgin syrup . . . sugar worthy the table of the gods.

—John Burroughs, *In the Catskills*

Maple-Walnut Oat Muffins

YIELD: 12 muffins

I LOVE OATS IN BREADS. The subtle oat flavor really shines here, reinforced beautifully by a sweet maple note. Very fragrant, these muffins will draw a crowd to your kitchen at any hour.

Ingredients

1¼ cups old-fashioned rolled oats
1 cup whole-wheat flour
½ cup unbleached all-purpose flour
1 teaspoon baking powder
1 teaspoon baking soda
1 teaspoon salt
2 eggs
1 cup buttermilk
½ cup pure maple syrup
¼ cup vegetable oil
½ cup finely chopped walnuts

1 Preheat the oven to 400°F/200°C. Grease a 12-cup muffin tin and set aside.

2 Process the oats in a food processor or blender until they are reduced to a coarse powder; it is fine if some larger flakes remain. Measure exactly 1 cup of the ground oats and combine it in a large bowl with the flours, baking powder, baking soda, and salt. Toss to mix.

3 Beat the eggs in a separate bowl, then blend in the buttermilk, maple syrup, and oil. Make a well in the dry ingredients, pour in the egg mixture, and stir, just to blend. Fold in the walnuts. Divide the batter evenly among the muffin cups.

4 Bake for 20 minutes, or until golden.

Flour Choice

If you want to replace some or all of the whole-wheat flour in these recipes with all-purpose flour, reduce the main liquid in the recipe slightly, because whole-wheat flour is more absorptive than white flour.

Maple Thoughts

In his essay "Phases of Farm Life," American naturalist John Burroughs says of sugar making, "Before the bud swells, before the grass springs, before the plow is started, comes the sugar harvest. It is the sequel of the bitter frost; a sap-run is the sweet good-by of winter."

Oven Apple Pancake

I'VE ALWAYS LOVED the rustic look of this pancake as much as I have the flavor. It's one of the prettier things you'll ever aim a jug of syrup at. Simple to make, too, for a fast breakfast or even a last-minute dessert. It puffs up beautifully in the oven but doesn't stay that way for long. You can serve this sliced, right from the skillet, or invert it onto a plate (first loosen underneath with a spatula).

Ingredients

- 2 firm cooking apples, peeled, cored, and sliced
- 2 tablespoons pure maple syrup
- 1 tablespoon lemon juice
- 4 tablespoons butter
- 3 eggs
- ½ cup milk or light cream
- ½ cup unbleached all-purpose flour
- ½ teaspoon ground cinnamon
- ¼ teaspoon salt
- Warm pure maple syrup for drizzling on top

1 Preheat the oven to 425°F/220°C. Toss the apples with the maple syrup and lemon juice and set aside. Melt the butter in a medium cast-iron skillet and remove from the heat.

2 Beat the eggs and milk in a bowl with 1 tablespoon of the melted butter. In a separate bowl, combine the flour, cinnamon, and salt, and whisk in the egg mixture until smooth.

3 Return the skillet to the heat and sauté the apples in the remaining butter over high heat. After 2 or 3 minutes, before they get mushy, spread the apples evenly in the skillet and slowly pour on the batter. Bake for 15 to 18 minutes, until very puffy and lightly browned. Serve hot or warm directly from the skillet, drizzled with maple syrup.

Banana Crêpes in Maple-Rum Sauce

WHETHER FOR A SPECIAL BREAKFAST, brunch, or even dessert, this recipe is easy to make. If the bananas are large, three should be enough. The bananas could be served plain, but the crêpes make for an elegant presentation. For dessert, instead of the crêpes, you can also serve the bananas on pound cake, topped with vanilla ice cream.

Ingredients

Crêpes

- 1 cup unbleached all-purpose flour
- 1¾ cups milk, plus more if needed
- 4 eggs
- 4 tablespoons butter, melted, plus 2⅔ tablespoons for greasing skillet
- ½ teaspoon salt

Bananas

- Butter for greasing skillet
- 4 small to medium bananas, peeled, halved lengthwise and then crosswise
- 2 tablespoons butter
- ⅓ cup pure maple syrup
- ¼ cup dark rum
- 1 tablespoon lemon juice

1 FOR THE CRÊPES: In a food processor or blender, process the flour, milk, eggs, butter, and salt until smooth. Add more milk if necessary; the batter should have the consistency of light cream. Chill for at least 30 minutes.

2 Heat a small nonstick skillet or crêpe pan over medium heat, then melt 1 teaspoon of butter in it. Spread the butter to cover the bottom and part of the sides of the pan.

3 Pour a little less than ¼ cup of the batter into the pan and quickly tip the pan, moving it in a circular fashion to evenly spread the batter over the bottom and sides. Cook for about 2 minutes; flip the crêpe and cook for 30 seconds longer.

4 Repeat with the remaining batter. As you finish cooking the crêpes, stack them between sheets of waxed paper to prevent them from sticking. (Crêpes may be frozen, unfilled; leave the waxed paper between them.)

5 FOR THE BANANAS: Preheat the oven to 375°F/190°C. Butter a large ovenproof skillet or casserole dish and lay the bananas in it, flat side down.

6 Melt the butter in a saucepan, then add the maple syrup. Bring to a boil, boil for a moment, then add the rum and lemon juice. As soon as the syrup returns to a boil, remove from the heat and pour over the bananas. Place in the oven and bake for 15 minutes, basting once or twice.

7 Remove the bananas from the oven. Using a slotted spatula, transfer two banana slices to a crêpe and roll the crêpe; place on a dish. Repeat with the remaining bananas to fill seven more crêpes (two per dish).

8 Put the skillet on a burner over high heat, or transfer the liquid to a saucepan if you used a casserole dish, and quickly reduce the liquid to a thick syrup. Spoon the sauce over the crêpes.

Pan-Fried Apple Rings

YIELD: 2–3 servings

HERE ARE THREE VERSIONS of apple rings: one plain, one saucy, and one crunchy. All are wonderful. They're sweet enough that, for breakfast, you wouldn't want to serve them with anything else sweet. They're best with breakfast meats, eggs, or yogurt. The crunchy version, with a graham cracker topping, could almost be considered a dessert, or a one-dish breakfast. Think of an apple crisp with lots of graham crackers in the topping; that's what it's like.

Ingredients

    1 large firm cooking apple, cored
    ½ cup water
    ⅓ cup pure maple syrup
    2 tablespoons butter

1 Trim a little off the ends of the apple, then cut the apple into slices a scant ½ inch thick; you'll have five or six slices. Set aside.

2 Heat the water, maple syrup, and butter in a large skillet. Stir to blend, bringing the mixture to a boil. When it reaches a boil, add the apple rings, in one layer.

3 Decrease the heat to a low to moderate boil and cook, uncovered, until the liquid is reduced to a thick syrup, turning the rings several times to glaze them. Watch that the apples don't get mushy and that the syrup doesn't burn. Transfer to a serving plate, scraping the remaining glaze over them. Serve hot or warm.

A Maple Lexicon

Ever wonder why maple syrup producers are called sugarmakers instead of syrup makers? It's because the product made from maple sap was most often maple sugar, until white sugar became more widely available and less expensive. Here are some other terms associated with the magic of converting sap to maple products:

Buddy. Used to describe the unpleasant taste of the sap that marks the end of the season.

Sugar bush. A grove of sugar maple trees; also called sugar grove or sugar orchard.

Sugar camp. Before the advent of tubing that carried sap to a central sugarhouse, maple-sugaring sites were often set up in remote areas in the woods by Native Americans and early settlers.

Sugarhouse. A simple building, usually uninsulated, that shelters the boiling setup for a sugar bush. Sugarhouses have a vent in the roof and space for an evaporator, fuel, and sap storage. Today, many sugarhouses have restaurants or gift shops attached so visitors can watch the sugaring operation. Besides promoting tourism, these operations help keep alive the uniquely North American tradition of sugar making.

Sugar-off. The end of the season, when the sap has stopped running and the boiling is done.

Apple Rings with
Maple Cream Sauce

1 Prepare and cook the apples as above. Before the syrup starts to coat the pan very thickly, transfer the rings to a warm plate, then pour ½ cup light cream into the pan. Bring to a boil and cook, stirring constantly, for 15 seconds.

2 Decrease the heat to an active simmer and cook, stirring, for a minute or two longer. The finished sauce will have the consistency of heavy cream. Be careful to avoid burning the sauce. Spoon the hot sauce over the rings and serve immediately.

Apple Rings with
Graham Cracker Crumb Topping

1 Before you begin, gently heat 2 tablespoons butter with 1 tablespoon maple syrup in a small saucepan, just until the butter melts. Stir in ¾ cup fine graham cracker crumbs; continue stirring until the mixture is smooth. Remove from the heat and set aside.

2 Preheat the oven broiler. Cook the apple rings as above. When heavily glazed, remove the pan from the heat and spread the reserved crumbs evenly over the apples. Broil briefly, just until the crumbs darken a shade or two. Watch carefully so the topping doesn't burn. Serve hot or warm.

Applejack-Spiked Baked Apples

YIELD: 4 servings

MOST BAKED APPLES I can take or leave, but these — lavishly bathed in a heady combination of applejack, maple, butter, and vanilla — are in a class by themselves. One of the important steps here is to cool the apples, periodically basting them with the thickening juices, before you serve them. Excellent with a dollop of cold sour cream or lightly sweetened whipped cream.

Ingredients

- ¼ cup finely chopped walnuts or pecans
- ¼ cup finely chopped dried dates
- 3 tablespoons butter
- 4 large firm cooking apples
- ⅓ cup pure maple syrup
- ¼ cup water
- ⅓ cup applejack or ⅔ cup apple cider reduced over low heat to ⅓ cup
- 1 teaspoon vanilla extract
- ¼ teaspoon ground cinnamon

1 Preheat the oven to 375°F/190°C. Combine the walnuts and dates in a small bowl. Rub about ½ tablespoon of the butter into the nut mixture so it all pulls together. Set aside.

2 Core the apples, a little on the wide side, then peel the upper third of each one; this will help prevent them from bursting. Cut ¹⁄₁₆ inch off the bottom of each apple, so they sit flat in the pan. Divide the reserved nut mixture among the cavities, stuffing it down into each one; hold one hand at the bottom so the mixture isn't pushed out. The filling should come to a little below the top of the apple, leaving a small space to hold the basting juice. Place the apples in a large pie plate.

3 Bring the maple syrup, water, and remaining 2½ tablespoons butter to a boil in a saucepan. Boil briefly, remove from the heat, then stir in the applejack, vanilla, and cinnamon. Pour this mixture over the apples, then put the pan in the oven. Bake for about 50 minutes, basting every 10 minutes or so. Remove from the oven and let cool, periodically basting with the pan juices as they thicken. Serve lukewarm, at room temperature, or — my favorite way — cold, for breakfast. Spoon any leftover juice over the apples when serving.

Breakfast Sweets

MAPLE MORNINGS

38

Lemon-Maple
Zucchini Bread

I'VE COME TO THINK OF zucchini bread recipes as the equivalent of those public service messages you hear on the radio: They're helpful, even though we have become indifferent to them by overexposure. But I do think this moist, maple variation is particularly good and definitely worth a try next time the annual summer zucchini invasion rolls around.

Ingredients

    3 eggs
    1 cup pure maple syrup
    ½ cup vegetable oil
    1 teaspoon vanilla extract
       Zest of 1 lemon, finely grated
  1½ cups grated zucchini or yellow summer squash
  1½ cups unbleached all-purpose flour
    1 cup whole-wheat flour
    1 tablespoon baking powder
    ½ teaspoon salt

1 Preheat the oven to 350°F/180°C. Grease a 5- by 9-inch loaf pan and set aside.

2 Beat the eggs with an electric mixer for 2 minutes. Gradually add the maple syrup, oil, vanilla, and lemon zest. Stir in the zucchini.

3 Combine the flours, baking powder, and salt in a large bowl. Make a well in the center, then stir in the zucchini mixture. Blend just until smooth, then turn into the prepared pan. Bake for 50 to 60 minutes, until a tester inserted into the center comes out clean. Let cool in the pan for 5 to 10 minutes, then remove from the pan and cool completely on a wire rack.

Breakfast Sweets

MAPLE MORNINGS

Maple-Cranberry-Nut Coffee Cake

YIELD: 1 large loaf

THE WISCONSIN MAPLE SYRUP Producer's Association, like many similar sugarmakers' organizations, offers recipes using maple syrup to show people that maple syrup is not just for pancakes. No wonder they chose this one — it's a keeper.

Ingredients

2¼ teaspoons active dry yeast
1 cup warm water (105–115°F/40–45°C)
¼ cup pure maple syrup
2 tablespoons vegetable oil
1 tablespoon buttermilk powder
1 teaspoon grated orange zest
1 teaspoon salt
3–3½ cups unbleached all-purpose flour
⅓ cup dried cranberries
⅓ cup walnuts, toasted and chopped

Maple Glaze

¼ cup pure maple syrup
2 tablespoons confectioners' sugar
1 tablespoon butter

1 Lightly oil a large bowl; set aside. In another large bowl, dissolve the yeast in the warm water. Add the maple syrup, oil, buttermilk powder, orange zest, and salt. Mix well.

2 Stir 1 cup of the flour into the mixture. Gradually stir in, ½ cup at a time, as much of the remaining flour as needed to make a soft dough. Blend in the cranberries and nuts. Knead for 5 to 10 minutes, until smooth.

3 Put the dough into the greased bowl, turning once to coat. Cover, set in a draft-free warm place, and let rise until doubled in bulk, about 1 hour.

4 Punch down the dough and turn it onto a lightly floured surface.

5 Shape it into a 6- by 14-inch oval using your hands or a rolling pin. Using a pizza cutter or sharp knife, make two slices to cut the dough lengthwise into three strips. Braid the strips; with water or milk, lightly moisten the ends to firmly attach them to each other.

6 Carefully place the braid on a nonstick or lightly oiled baking sheet. Cover with a clean, light-weight cloth; let rise until doubled in bulk, about 45 minutes.

7 Preheat the oven to 350°F/180°C. Uncover the braid and bake for 25 to 30 minutes, until lightly browned. Let cool slightly.

8 TO MAKE THE GLAZE: Combine the maple syrup, confectioners' sugar, and butter in a small saucepan. Bring to a boil, stirring, to form a smooth, spreadable glaze. Frost the warm loaf with the glaze or with Maple Butter Frosting (page 155).

Note: This dough can be prepared in a bread machine. Make sure all the ingredients are at room temperature; add the ingredients in the order specified in the owner's manual for your bread machine. Add the fruit and nuts at the appropriate time for your machine. Set the bread machine on the dough cycle. Allow the machine to run its cycle, adding flour and water to adjust the dough as needed. Continue with steps 5 through 8 to complete the bread.

Golden Cornmeal Cake

YIELD: 12 or more servings

HERE'S A SPECIAL-OCCASION breakfast cake worth rolling out of bed for. Sometimes I decrease the amount of coconut and add chopped walnuts.

Ingredients

- 1 cup (2 sticks) butter, softened
- 1 cup pure maple syrup, at room temperature
- 3 eggs, at room temperature
- 2 teaspoons vanilla extract
- Zest of 1 orange, finely grated
- 1¼ cups unbleached all-purpose flour
- ¾ cup cornmeal, preferably stone-ground
- 1 tablespoon baking powder
- ½ teaspoon salt
- 1½ cups sweetened shredded coconut
- ¾ cup sour cream
- 1 cup raisins

1 Preheat the oven to 350°F/180°C. Grease a large tube pan or a 10-inch Bundt pan and set aside.

2 Cream the butter with an electric mixer, gradually adding the maple syrup. Beat in the eggs, one at a time, then the vanilla and orange zest.

3 In a separate bowl, sift the flour, cornmeal, baking powder, and salt. Toss in the coconut. Add the dry ingredients to the butter mixture alternately with the sour cream, in two or three stages, each time stirring just to blend. Don't beat it. Fold in the raisins. Bake for 50 to 60 minutes, until a tester inserted into the center comes out clean. Let cool briefly in the pan, then turn onto a plate.

Mapled Yogurt

You don't have to cook to enjoy maple's goodness for breakfast. Simply stir a tablespoon or two of pure maple syrup into a bowl of plain or vanilla yogurt and top with a sprinkling of granola, chopped fresh fruit, raisins, dried cranberries, chopped nuts, wheat germ, or even chocolate chips.

Maple Bread Pudding

BILL SCHNEIDER of Browning Brook Maple submitted this stovetop version of bread pudding to the Massachusetts Maple Producers Association when it got together to publish recipes featuring pure maple syrup from the Bay State. It's a great breakfast dish, or even dessert, especially when your oven is in use for another item on your menu.

Ingredients

- ¾ cup pure maple syrup
- 1 tablespoon butter, softened
- 4 thick slices bread, crusts trimmed
- ½ cup chopped walnuts, pecans, or raisins
- 1 teaspoon lemon juice
- 2 cups milk
- 2 eggs
- ¼ teaspoon salt
- ¼ teaspoon vanilla extract

1 Pour the maple syrup into the top of a double boiler. Butter each slice of bread, then cut into cubes. Add the bread to the syrup, along with the nuts and lemon juice.

2 In a medium bowl, beat the milk, eggs, salt, and vanilla and pour over the bread mixture. Do not stir, but press the bread down with a fork so that it is thoroughly moistened.

3 Bring water in the bottom of the double boiler to a gentle boil; set the top pan over the boiling water and cook, uncovered, for 1 hour to 1 hour 15 minutes, until a knife inserted into the top of the pudding comes out clean. Add more boiling water to the bottom pan as needed.

4 The pudding makes its own sauce; spoon it over each serving.

Winter Squash Spoon Bread

SOMEWHERE BETWEEN a soufflé and corn bread, spoon bread is based on a thick sauce known as a rick. Here, I put puréed winter squash — acorn, butternut, or even pumpkin — into the rick with a little maple syrup. This puffs up nicely, but it doesn't stay that way for long once it comes out of the oven. It is very good cold, for breakfast, with a little cream and maple syrup drizzled over it. But it's also a fine hot accompaniment to poultry dishes.

Ingredients

- 1½ cups peeled and diced winter squash (½-inch pieces)
- ⅓ cup pure maple syrup
- 2 cups milk
- 1 cup cornmeal, preferably stone-ground
- ¾ teaspoon salt
- ⅛ teaspoon ground nutmeg
- 4 tablespoons butter, cut into ½-inch pieces
- 5 eggs, separated

1 Preheat the oven to 375°F/190°C. Grease a large shallow casserole dish and set aside.

2 Put the squash into a large saucepan with plenty of water. Bring to a boil, cover, then simmer until the squash is very soft, about 20 minutes. Drain in a colander for several minutes, then purée the squash with the maple syrup in a food processor or blender. Set aside.

3 Pour the milk into a large pot. Gradually whisk in the cornmeal over low heat. Turn the heat to medium-high and cook the cornmeal, stirring, until it starts to thicken, 3 to 5 minutes. Decrease the heat slightly and continue to stir and cook until it is quite thick, several minutes longer.

4 Stir in the salt, nutmeg, butter, and squash mixture; whisk until smooth. Remove from the heat and whisk in the egg yolks. Pour into a large bowl.

5 Beat the egg whites until stiff, then fold them into the squash mixture. Pour into the prepared casserole and bake for about 35 minutes, or until golden and puffed; large cracks will appear on the surface.

Lacy Sweet-Potato Patties

THESE SAVORY PANCAKES are designed to be served with just a drizzle of maple syrup, so they're a good choice when you're not in the mood for an overly sweet breakfast. They go well with almost any egg dish, a side of applesauce, breakfast meats, toast, and biscuits. The pancake mixture isn't terribly cohesive, but as long as you don't manhandle the patties or make them overly huge, they'll hold together just fine.

Ingredients

- 1 large sweet potato, peeled (about ½ pound)
- ¼ teaspoon salt, plus more as needed
- 1 egg
- 2 tablespoons heavy or light cream
- 1 tablespoon cornmeal
- ½ cup minced ham or Canadian bacon
- 1 tablespoon minced onion
- Freshly ground black pepper
- Vegetable oil for frying
- Butter for frying

1 Remove any bad spots from the potato, then grate it into a bowl. Mix in the salt and set aside for 5 minutes.

2 While that sits, beat the egg lightly in a large bowl, then whisk in the cream and cornmeal. Using your hands, squeeze the moisture out of the grated potato, then add the potato to the egg mixture. Stir in the ham, onion, and salt and pepper to taste.

3 Heat about 1 tablespoon of oil in a heavy skillet over medium heat. Add 1 tablespoon of butter, let it melt, then spoon the mixture into the skillet. Use about ¼ cup of the mixture per pancake, and don't crowd the pancakes. Spread and flatten the patties with a fork to a thickness of about ¼ inch. They should be no wider than your spatula. Fry until dark and crusty on the outside, 3 to 4 minutes per side, flipping only once. Serve hot. The patties hold up for a little while in a hot oven, if you want to serve them all at once.

Breakfast Savories

MAPLE MORNINGS

Maple-Bacon Strata

YIELD: 8 servings

WHEN DIANNE CUTILLO, my previous editor at Storey Publishing, invites friends over for brunch, this is one of her guests' favorites. You'll need to begin preparing it a day ahead.

Ingredients

- ½ pound bacon, chopped into ¼-inch pieces
- 1¼ cups heavy cream
- 1 cup milk
- ½ cup pure maple syrup
- 5 eggs
- 1 teaspoon Dijon mustard
- 1 teaspoon crumbled dried sage
- 1 teaspoon salt
- 8 slices (each 1 inch thick) sweet Portuguese bread or challah, lightly toasted and cut into thirds
- 3 cups grated sharp cheddar cheese
- ⅔ cup chopped pistachio nuts

1 Grease a 2-quart casserole dish and set aside.

2 Cook the bacon pieces in a medium skillet over medium-high heat until they are crisp, about 10 minutes. Drain on paper towels. Set aside.

3 Whisk together the cream, milk, maple syrup, eggs, mustard, sage, and salt in a bowl. Set aside.

4 Lay half of the bread in the prepared casserole dish. Sprinkle it with half of the bacon, half of the cheese, and half of the nuts. Continue layering with the remaining ingredients.

5 Pour the egg mixture over the layers, cover, and refrigerate overnight.

6 Remove the casserole from the refrigerator 30 minutes before baking. Preheat the oven to 350°F/180°C. Uncover the dish and bake for about 40 minutes, or until bubbly and golden.

7 Remove from the oven and let stand for 10 minutes before serving.

Fried Mush/Polenta

I LOVE CORNY THINGS, and these luscious slices — dredged in cinnamon-spiked cornmeal, delicately fried in butter, then doused with maple syrup — are high on my list of breakfast favorites. They're perfect with breakfast meats and eggs, or with applesauce, berries, or yogurt on the side. A few other things to know: You must start this the night before. This will keep in the refrigerator for several days, so you can slice and fry anytime. And be sure to use fresh, stone-ground cornmeal, available in health food stores.

Ingredients

- 4 cups water
- 1 teaspoon salt
- 2 cups stone-ground cornmeal
- 3 tablespoons butter
- 1½ teaspoons ground cinnamon
  Pure maple syrup for drizzling on top

1 Grease a large shallow casserole dish, measuring either 8 by 12 inches or 9 by 13 inches.

2 Heat the water in a large pot. Add the salt. As the water heats, sprinkle in 1½ cups of the cornmeal, a little at a time, whisking all the while. When the mixture reaches a boil, switch to a wooden spoon. Decrease the heat to medium-low and cook the mush, stirring continuously, for 15 minutes; the mixture will become quite thick. Stir in 1 tablespoon of the butter until melted, then remove from the heat.

3 Immediately scrape the mush into the prepared casserole and flatten the top as best you can with a spatula. Let cool to room temperature, cover, and refrigerate overnight.

4 The next morning, stir the cinnamon into the remaining ½ cup cornmeal. Cut the chilled cornmeal mush into serving-size pieces — roughly 2 by 3 inches is a good size, but anywhere thereabouts is fine. Melt the remaining 2 tablespoons butter in a cast-iron skillet over medium-low heat. Dredge the slices in the cinnamon-cornmeal mix, then fry them in the butter, without crowding, 3 to 4 minutes on each side. Serve hot, drizzled with maple syrup.

Birch Buckets

Sap buckets in one form or another have been used in the collection of maple sap for some three hundred years. One early observer of the Native Americans describes their sap buckets, which were "fashioned from birch bark, cut and folded at the corners . . . and seamed with pine resin. The buckets were of various sizes, though usually held from 1 to 2 gallons."

Maple-Onion Marmalade

YIELD: About 2 cups

WHETHER YOU CALL THIS a marmalade, relish, or French confit, these slow-cooked, sweet-and-sour onions make a great garnish for roasts, burgers, omelets, grilled cheese sandwiches, and about a thousand other things. I especially like this as a garnish for the Bacon and Egg Waffle Sandwich on page 50. If this recipe makes more than you'll eat within a couple of weeks, divide the mixture between two jars and give one of them to a friend.

Ingredients

- 3 tablespoons light olive oil
- 6 cups halved and thinly sliced sweet onions (3–4 large)
- ½ teaspoon salt, plus more as needed
- ¼ cup plus 1 tablespoon pure maple syrup
- ¼ cup apple cider vinegar
- ¼ cup water
- ¼ teaspoon freshly ground black pepper
- ¼ teaspoon dried thyme
- 1 bay leaf

1 Heat the oil in a very large skillet. Add the onions and salt. Sauté over fairly high heat for 5 minutes, stirring often. Decrease the heat to low, cover the skillet, and cook the onions for 10 minutes, stirring several times. Remove the cover and continue to cook the onions over medium heat until they're quite soft and turning golden brown, about 5 minutes.

2 Stir the maple syrup, vinegar, and water together in a small bowl. Add the liquid to the onions along with the pepper, thyme, and bay leaf. Continue to cook the onions, stirring often, until nearly all the liquid evaporates and the remaining liquid is syrupy. Remove from the heat. Add a little more salt, if needed. Remove the bay leaf.

3 Spoon the marmalade into one or two clean jars. Let cool completely, then screw on the lids and refrigerate. This will keep for 2 or more weeks in the refrigerator.

Bacon and Egg Waffle Sandwich

TRICKED-OUT BREAKFAST
sandwiches have become all the rage in recent years, from fast food joints to hip neighborhood eateries. And why not? It's fun to venture from the standard-issue bacon and eggs on occasion, especially when the payoff is this good. The magic here happens when two cheeses, one salty and one smoky, encounter bacon and sweet maple, creating a sweet-smoky-salty harmony that'll make your taste buds sing. Even without the onion marmalade garnish, this would be a triumph; with it, this open-face sandwich is in a class of its own. (The recipe makes two sandwiches. Scale it up, as required.)

Ingredients

- 4 slices bacon
- 1 tablespoon butter, plus a little softened butter for the waffles
  Pinch of salt
- 4 eggs, lightly beaten
- 2 waffles (freshly made or prepared frozen)
  Warm pure maple syrup for drizzling
- ½ cup crumbled feta cheese
- ½ cup grated smoked cheddar or smoked Gouda cheese
- 2 tablespoons Maple-Onion Marmalade (page 49), optional but highly recommended

1 Preheat your oven's broiler and line a small baking sheet with aluminum foil.

2 Cook the bacon in a large skillet, preferably nonstick, over medium heat until crisp. Set the bacon aside on paper towels. Drain the fat from the pan and wipe it out with paper towels, then put the pan back on the heat.

3 Melt the butter in the skillet. Add a pinch or two of salt to the eggs, then add the eggs to the skillet and cook them to your liking; slightly soft is best. Remove the pan from the heat, cover it, and set aside.

4 Toast the waffles if using frozen. Transfer the waffles to the prepared baking sheet. Spread a little butter on each one, then drizzle with a little maple syrup, keeping it in the cavities. Top each waffle with 2 slices of bacon, then divide the eggs between the waffles, making a slightly flattened mound on each one. Divide the feta between them, then top with the cheddar.

5 Run the sandwiches under the broiler, just until the cheese melts; this should take only a minute or two. Keep a close eye on them. Transfer the sandwiches to serving plates and top each one with a tablespoon or so of the onion marmalade, if desired.

Canadian Bacon Cheese Dream

YIELD: 2 servings

READING THROUGH some old James Beard columns, I came across a reference to a once popular sandwich he called a Cheese Dream — a combination of cheddar cheese, sliced tomato, and bacon. Inspired by that thought, I spun off this breakfast version, and let me tell you, our friends with the golden arches have nothing on this. If your tomatoes aren't garden fresh, they might benefit from a quick flash in the pan with the bacon.

Ingredients

- 1½ tablespoons pure maple syrup
- 1 tablespoon water
- 2 teaspoons lemon juice or apple cider vinegar
- 1½ teaspoons Dijon mustard
- Pinch of ground cloves
- Pinch of cayenne pepper
- 1 tablespoon butter
- 2 thick slices Canadian bacon
- 1 English muffin, halved and toasted
- 2 eggs, fried over hard
- 2 thick slices tomato
- 1 cup grated cheddar cheese, preferably smoked

1 In a small bowl, whisk together the maple syrup, water, lemon juice, mustard, cloves, and cayenne.

2 Melt the butter in a heavy skillet over medium heat and add the bacon. Fry gently, about 1 minute per side, then pour in the sauce. Increase the heat and continue to cook until the liquid is reduced to a thick glaze. Remove from the heat.

3 Preheat the broiler. Place the toasted muffin halves in a pie plate. Swish the bacon slices in the glaze, then lay a slice on each muffin half. Top each with a fried egg and a slice of tomato, then spread the cheese over the top. Broil just until the cheese melts. Serve at once.

Breakfast Savories

MAPLE MORNINGS

52

Maple Butter

YIELD: About ¾ cup

TRADITIONAL MAPLE BUTTER, more commonly called maple cream, requires heating syrup to just the right temperature, cooling it to just the right temperature, then beating it to a creamy, thick consistency. This simpler version still makes a delicious spread for toast, muffins, and sweet breads.

Ingredients
- ½ cup (1 stick) butter, softened
- Pinch of salt
- ¼ cup pure maple syrup

1 In a food processor or with an electric mixer, whip the butter and salt until light and fluffy.

2 With the motor running, slowly pour the maple syrup through the feed tube of the food processor, running the processor until the syrup is well incorporated. (If using an electric mixer, dribble the syrup into the butter while beating constantly.) Adding the syrup slowly and beating constantly will prevent the mixture from separating. The spread may be refrigerated, in a covered container, for up to 3 weeks.

Where to Tap?

Among sugarmakers, there's no dearth of down-home wisdom regarding the placement of taps — "the higher (or lower) the tap, the sweeter the sap"; "tap the warm side of the tree"; "the older the tree, the sweeter the sap" — but studies have shown that tap location has little or no appreciable effect on yield. With each successive year, the position of new tapholes is staggered, to avoid hitting old tapholes or dead tissue, hidden by new bark, that may contribute to a reduced sap flow.

Breakfast Extras

MAPLE MORNINGS

53

Pineapple-Peach Butter

PINEAPPLES AND PEACHES,
I think, are two fruits that combine especially well with maple, and that's why I like this butter. Use it to top vanilla ice cream or pancakes. Or stir it into plain yogurt for a quick, intense fruit lift.

Ingredients

- 3 pounds ripe peaches
- 2 20-ounce cans unsweetened crushed pineapple
- ½ cup water
- ¼ cup lemon juice (from about 2 lemons)
- 1 cinnamon stick
- ½ cup pure maple syrup

1 Bring a medium pot of water to a boil. Drop in the peaches, several at a time, and let the water come back to a boil. Boil for 15 seconds, then remove the peaches with a slotted spoon. Repeat for all the peaches.

2 When cool enough to handle, slip off the skins and cut the peach flesh into chunks. Transfer to a large nonreactive pot and add the pineapple and its juice, water, lemon juice, and cinnamon stick. Bring to a boil over medium heat. Decrease the heat, cover partially, and simmer gently, stirring occasionally, until the peaches are very soft, about 30 minutes. Remove from the heat and take out the cinnamon stick.

3 Preheat the oven to 350°F/180°C.

4 Purée the fruit in a food processor or blender. Add the maple syrup and pulse to combine. Scrape the mixture into a large nonreactive casserole dish.

5 Bake for as long as 2 hours, stirring occasionally, until the mixture is reduced by about half.

6 Refrigerate, tightly covered, for up to 4 weeks. If desired, pack the butter into four half-pint, sterilized canning jars and process for 10 minutes in a boiling-water bath according to the instructions provided by the manufacturer of the jar.

Maple–Cream Cheese Spread

YIELD: About 1 cup

REDUCING MAPLE SYRUP by cooking it before combining it with cream cheese prevents the mixture from separating. The Maine Maple Producers Association, which created this recipe, says that this spread can be stored, refrigerated and tightly covered, "for a long time — if it lasts." It doesn't last long in my house.

Ingredients

- ½ cup pure maple syrup
- 6 ounces cream cheese, softened

1 Simmer the maple syrup in a small saucepan over medium-low heat, stirring occasionally, until it is thickened to the texture of heavy honey, about 235°F/115°C on a candy thermometer. Do not overcook, or the syrup will not mix smoothly into the cream cheese.

2 Let the maple syrup cool slightly, stirring once or twice, then beat it into the cream cheese. Store tightly covered in the refrigerator.

Using Flavored Butter and Cream Cheese

Maple butter and maple cream cheese lift everyday foods out of the ordinary, so don't limit their use to breads, bagels, and crackers. Here are some ideas to inspire:

- Stir dried cranberries or raisins or chopped dried apricots, apples, pineapple, or dates into maple butter or maple cream cheese and spread on celery or crackers.
- Spread maple butter or maple cream cheese on apple or pear slices for a healthier alternative to cheese and crackers. Dip the fruit into a bowl of water containing 2 tablespoons of lemon juice to prevent browning.
- Create sandwich sensations: Use maple cream cheese instead of mayonnaise on a turkey sandwich. How about a maple butter and jelly sandwich?
- Instead of a rich sauce, top broiled fish, chicken, or pork with a dab of maple butter.

Creamy Maple–Peanut Butter Sauce

YIELD: 1–1¼ cups

NOTHING THIS SIMPLE should be so delicious and versatile, but it is. We use this creamy sauce on pancakes and waffles, over granola, or on ice cream, many cakes, hot cereals, muffins, sliced bananas — anywhere a thick peanut butter and maple emulsion would be at home. Using the blender gives you the best consistency: thick and light. This will keep nicely in the fridge, but you'll probably have to whisk in a bit of water, no more than a teaspoon at a time, to smooth it out when you use it.

Ingredients

- ¾ cup smooth peanut butter
- ⅓ cup pure maple syrup
- ⅓ cup water
- Lemon juice as needed
- Pinch of salt

1 Combine the peanut butter, maple syrup, and water in a blender. Blend until the mixture is smooth and creamy, and has a fairly thick consistency. It should either stick to a spoon or fall off in thick clumps. Stop the blender and scrape down the sides with a rubber spatula, if necessary.

2 Taste the sauce, adding a bit of lemon juice, ½ teaspoon at a time, and a pinch of salt to perk up the flavor. Transfer to a storage jar or small bowl, cover, and refrigerate.

The moon, though slight, was moon enough to show
On every tree a bucket with a lid

— Robert Frost, "Evening in a Sugar Orchard"

Blushing Applesauce

FRESH CRANBERRIES give this delicious applesauce its pretty blush, and it's not the only thing that'll be blushing when the compliments start to fly. This is an autumn staple around our home, just right for breakfast with muffins, scones, or pancakes, or as a light evening dessert, topped with a spoonful of yogurt or lightly sweetened sour cream.

Ingredients

4–5 large apples, peeled, cored, and coarsely chopped
¾ cup fresh or frozen cranberries
1 cup water
¼ cup pure maple syrup
2 tablespoons sugar
Pinch of salt
1 tablespoon lemon juice
⅛ teaspoon ground cinnamon

1 Put the apples, cranberries, water, maple syrup, sugar, and salt in a large nonreactive stovetop casserole. Bring to a boil, cover, then decrease the heat to a low boil. Cook the apples, tightly covered, until tender, about 15 minutes. Check the water level after 10 minutes, to make sure there's still plenty of liquid in the pot. When the apples are tender, remove them from the heat. Transfer the fruit and liquid to a bowl and let cool thoroughly. (The fruit can be covered with plastic wrap and refrigerated until the next day, if you like, before processing.)

2 Transfer the fruit and liquid to the bowl of a food processor. Add the lemon juice and cinnamon. Process the fruit to make a saucy texture, leaving it slightly chunky or smooth — however you prefer it. Transfer to jars, seal, and refrigerate until ready to serve.

Measuring Tip

Syrup often sticks to the sides of measuring cups and spoons. To make it easier to measure and pour (and to waste less), grease the cup or spoon lightly or coat with vegetable cooking spray before measuring.

Maple Hot Chocolate

PROPERLY SPEAKING, hot chocolate is made with melted chocolate and hot cocoa is made with cocoa powder, though many folks use the terms interchangeably. Whatever way you like it, maple makes it more special.

Ingredients

- 1 cup milk, preferably whole
- 2 ounces (2 squares) semisweet or bittersweet chocolate
- 1 teaspoon pure maple syrup
- Whipped cream or marshmallow crème, optional

1 Heat the milk and chocolate in the top of a double boiler over simmering water until the chocolate is melted and well incorporated; do not boil.

2 Remove from the heat; stir in the maple syrup. Pour into a mug or two small cups and top with whipped cream, if desired.

Maple-Yogurt Smoothie

YIELD: 2 servings

ALMOST UNLIMITED possibilities, of course, abound for maple smoothies. I've used bananas here, but soft berries in season are also terrific; any soft fruit will work. You can make spiked versions by adding a compatible spirit or liqueur — Kahlúa would be good in this version, for instance. Let your imagination guide you, bearing in mind the proportions of yogurt to maple and fruit.

Ingredients

- 1 cup plain yogurt
- ½ cup milk
- ⅓ cup pure maple syrup
- 1 ripe banana, peeled
- Pinch of ground cinnamon
- Several ice cubes, crushed

1 Combine the yogurt, milk, maple syrup, banana, and cinnamon in a blender.

2 Add the crushed ice and process until smooth. It's fine if shards of ice remain after the blending. Serve at once.

Note: To crush the ice cubes, put them in the folds of a kitchen towel and shatter with a hammer.

Syrup by the Numbers

Some people find the price difference between pure maple syrup and maple-flavored pancake syrup (generally 98 to 100 percent corn syrup) startling. Thinking about what it takes to produce the real thing puts that into perspective.

It takes four maple trees, at least 40 years old, to yield enough sap in 6 weeks to produce 1 gallon of maple syrup. Think about collecting and transporting that sap to the sugar-house for boiling.

It takes about 40 gallons of sap, boiled down in an evaporator, to produce 1 gallon of syrup. On a smaller scale, that means it takes 2 gallons of sap to produce 1 cup of syrup. Comparing that to milk, that's two big jugs of milk to make one school-lunch milk carton.

It takes about one cord of wood or 60 gallons of oil to boil 800 gallons of syrup. Depending on the size of the evaporator used, that would require anywhere from 2 hours to 2 days.

Lemon-Lime Herbal Cooler

I DRINK GALLONS of this sort of thing in the summertime. There's a lot of flexibility here as far as what kind of herbal tea you can use. Lemon is probably my favorite, but I've also used orange- and raspberry-flavored herbal teas, and chamomile and peppermint, too. Don't let the tea steep for more than five minutes, or you'll overpower the maple flavor.

Ingredients

    2 quarts water
    8 bags lemon or other herbal tea
¾–1 cup pure maple syrup
    ¼ cup lime juice (from about 2 medium limes)
       Fresh mint sprigs, if available
       Ice cubes (approximately 2 cups)

1 Bring the water to a boil in a kettle or pot. Put the tea bags in a large heatproof bowl and pour in the water. Steep for 5 minutes, and then remove the tea bags with a slotted spoon.

2 Stir in the maple syrup, lime juice, and mint, and let cool to room temperature. Remove the mint and transfer the liquid to a large jug. Cover and refrigerate if not serving immediately. Add the ice cubes shortly before serving.

Maple Sap Coffee

Many a sugarmaker prepares coffee with raw maple sap, which Native Americans called "maple water," because it imparts a slightly sweet maple taste to the coffee. For the same reason, maple sap can also be used to make wine and beer.

Fruit-Flavored Syrup

YIELD: About 1½ cups

THERE'S NOTHING WRONG with drizzling pure maple syrup over ice cream, pound cake, pancakes, or waffles, but infusing the syrup with fruit flavor brings out the best of both. This is one area where it's easy to be creative. Mix and match the fruit and optional ingredients to create a signature syrup.

Ingredients

- 2 cups chopped ripe fruit (pears, pineapple, peaches, plums, or apricots) or 2 cups berries (raspberries, blueberries, or strawberries)
- 1 cup pure maple syrup
- 1 teaspoon finely grated peeled fresh gingerroot or 1 vanilla bean, split in half lengthwise, optional

1 In a food processor or blender, process the fruit, maple syrup, and gingerroot, if desired, until the mixture is puréed.

2 Pour the mixture into a small saucepan. If using the vanilla bean, scrape the seeds into the mixture. Simmer over low heat for 5 minutes.

3 Using a fine-mesh sieve or a double layer of cheesecloth in a strainer, strain the syrup, pressing the fruit with the back of a spoon to extract as much liquid as possible. Serve immediately or refrigerate and reheat before serving.

three

Beyond Breakfast

f you need proof that maple adds magic to just about any food, look no further. Whether in a spicy soup, a tangy salad, or a barbecue sauce, the flavor of maple will enliven your taste buds. And maple syrup combined with the gifts of the garden makes for exceptional side dishes.

In main dishes, maple is less likely to be used as a sweetener than as a distinctive ingredient on its own. You'll love how it pairs with ingredients such as vinegar, citrus juice, pepper, and strong spices, filling your lunch, dinner, and snack plates with flavor.

Sweet Potato and Bacon Bisque

YIELD: 4–6 servings

WHAT A WONDERFUL cold-weather soup this is! The maple lifts the sweetness and flavor of the sweet potatoes, while the bacon and onion add depth and contrast. Excellent with corn bread or corn muffins and a mixed green salad served with a mustard vinaigrette.

Ingredients

  4 cups peeled and diced sweet potatoes
  4 cups water
  6 slices bacon
  1 small onion, minced
1½ cups light cream or milk
  ¼ cup pure maple syrup
  1 teaspoon salt, plus more as needed
  ¼ teaspoon ground cinnamon
    Sour cream for serving, optional

1 Bring the sweet potatoes and water to a boil in a large soup pot. Cover the pot, decrease the heat, and simmer until the potatoes are very tender, about 20 minutes. Remove from the heat.

2 While the potatoes are cooking, sauté the bacon in a skillet until crisp. Remove from the pan; blot with paper towels. Pour off all but about 3 tablespoons of fat, then add the onion and sauté for 5 minutes. Remove from the heat.

3 Working in batches, purée the potatoes and cooking water in a food processor or blender. (Always be careful when puréeing hot liquids in a blender. Never fill the container more than one-third full to avoid the risk of the lid blowing off.) Return the purée to the soup pot, then stir in the onion, cream, maple syrup, salt, and cinnamon. Crumble the bacon and add that to the pot. Heat, but do not boil, and serve piping hot. Put a small dollop of sour cream in each bowl, if desired.

Creamy Maple Fondue

WHETHER YOU SERVE THIS as a first course, on an hors d'oeuvres buffet, or for dessert, fondue is a delicious way to savor maple. It's another recipe from a member of the Citadelle Maple Syrup Producers' Cooperative in Quebec.

Ingredients

- ½ cup pure maple syrup
- 2 tablespoons cornstarch
- 2½ cups light cream or crème fraîche
- 2–3 cups firm fruits and berries, cut into small pieces

1 Gently heat the maple syrup in a small saucepan for 5 minutes.

2 Mix the cornstarch with 2 tablespoons of the cream in a small bowl.

3 In a medium saucepan, bring the remaining cream to a simmer over medium heat; add the maple syrup. Whisk the cornstarch mixture into the cream mixture and cook, stirring continuously, until it comes to a boil. Boil while stirring for about 1 minute.

4 Serve the fondue in a small pan over a spirit lamp. Arrange the fruit and fondue forks or skewers around the fondue.

Sugaring-Off Party

Friends and neighbors often gathered, out in the woods at the sugar camp or sugarhouse in many cases, to celebrate the end of the maple-sugaring season, a tradition still observed by many sugarmakers.

Lots of maple syrup is served, along with freshly made maple cream and taffy. Other foods customarily served at the gatherings include maple-glazed ham, and doughnuts for dipping in the fresh syrup, along with pickles, to counter all the sweetness.

Soups & Starters

BEYOND BREAKFAST

Curried Pumpkin-Apple Soup

DIANNE CUTILLO says her passion for maple syrup grew immensely while working on this book. Inspired by her new maple mania, she revised this recipe. More like "transformed," she reports. The maple mellows the curry, and together they accent pumpkin beautifully. Dianne's family and friends love the maple version. Why am I not surprised?

Ingredients

- 4 tablespoons butter
- 1 cup chopped Vidalia onion
- 1 small apple (Braeburn or Granny Smith), peeled, cored, and coarsely chopped
- 2 cloves garlic, crushed
- 1 teaspoon curry powder
- ½ teaspoon salt
- ¼ teaspoon ground coriander
- ⅛ teaspoon red pepper flakes
- 2 cups chicken broth
- 1 cup apple cider
- 2 cups pumpkin purée
- 1 cup light cream or half-and-half
- ¼ cup pure maple syrup

1 Melt the butter in a large saucepan over medium-high heat. Add the onion, apple, and garlic, and sauté until soft, about 5 minutes. Add the curry powder, salt, coriander, and red pepper; cook for 1 minute.

2 Add the broth and cider and boil gently, uncovered, for 15 to 20 minutes.

3 Stir in the pumpkin, cream, and maple syrup; cook for 5 minutes.

4 In a food processor or blender, purée the soup in three or four batches. (Always be careful when puréeing hot liquids in a blender. Never fill the container more than one-third full to avoid the risk of the lid blowing off.) Return the soup to the pot and cook over very low heat for 5 minutes; do not boil.

5 Ladle the soup into four bowls and serve piping hot.

Slow Cooker Sweet-and-Sour Meatballs, Yankee-Style

YIELD: 10 or more appetizer servings

SWEET AND TANGY, the secret ingredient in these thickly sauced meatballs isn't just the maple syrup; it's also the jellied cranberry sauce (but make them guess before you tell them). I like to throw these in the slow cooker on a weekend morning so they're ready when the football games start later in the day. A tailgate and potluck classic, these travel and reheat well. For the sake of convenience, I've called for frozen, fully cooked meatballs. You can, of course, substitute homemade ones. Serve them alone or with little slider rolls.

Ingredients

- 1 (12-ounce) bottle plus ½ cup chili sauce, preferably Heinz
- 1 (14-ounce) can plus ½ cup jellied cranberry sauce (not the whole-berry variety)
- 1 medium onion, finely chopped
- ⅓ cup pure maple syrup
- 2 tablespoons firmly packed brown sugar
- 2 teaspoons Worcestershire sauce
- ½ teaspoon smoked paprika
- ¼ teaspoon cayenne pepper
- 1½–2 pounds (50 to 60 bite-size) frozen fully cooked meatballs
- ¼ cup cranberry or grape juice, optional

---

1 In a large saucepan, combine the chili sauce, cranberry sauce, onion, maple syrup, brown sugar, Worcestershire, paprika, and cayenne. Gradually bring to a simmer, whisking well to break up the cranberry jelly and smooth out the sauce.

2 Pour the sauce into a large slow cooker and add the meatballs. Stir well. Cover and cook on high for 3 to 4 hours, stirring from time to time. The sauce will be nice and thick, but if you want to thin it slightly or tone it down, add the cranberry juice, a tablespoon or so at a time, as the meatballs cook.

Maple-Glazed Chicken Wings

YIELD: 4–6 appetizer servings

THE CHILI SAUCE in this marinade from the Citadelle cooperative provides a nice contrast to the maple's sweetness. The wings are good out of the oven, but I also like them grilled (over medium-high heat, turning frequently, until thoroughly cooked).

Ingredients

- 1 small onion, chopped
- ½ cup pure maple syrup
- 5 tablespoons chili sauce
- 2 tablespoons apple cider vinegar
- 1 tablespoon prepared mustard
- 1 teaspoon Worcestershire sauce
- 2½ pounds chicken wings (about 18)

1 Combine the onion, maple syrup, chili sauce, vinegar, mustard, and Worcestershire in a shallow dish.

2 Add the chicken wings to the dish, turn to coat, and marinate for at least 4 hours in the refrigerator, keeping them covered and turning occasionally. (The wings can be marinated for up to 2 days.)

3 Preheat the oven to 400°F/200°C. Arrange the wings in a shallow baking pan so they are not touching one another. Discard the remaining marinade.

4 Bake for 20 to 30 minutes, until golden and crispy, turning the wings every 5 minutes to make sure they brown evenly.

Orange-Maple Wings

SOAKING CHICKEN WINGS in this buttermilk-orange-maple bath makes the meat butter-tender and infuses it with sweetness. The flavor here is delicate and subtle, so serve them with buttered noodles or another simple side.

Ingredients

- 1½ cups buttermilk
- ⅓ cup pure maple syrup
- 2 oranges, peeled and sectioned
- 1 teaspoon ground cinnamon
- 2–2½ pounds chicken wings (about 18)

1 Mix the buttermilk and maple syrup in a large bowl.

2 Briefly process the orange sections and cinnamon in a food processor or blender to make a coarse purée.

3 Stir the orange mixture into the buttermilk, then add the chicken wings. Stir to coat. Cover and refrigerate for at least 1 hour or up to 24 hours, stirring every now and then.

4 Preheat the oven to 400°F/200°C. Arrange the wings in a shallow baking pan so they are not touching one another.

5 Bake for 20 to 30 minutes, until golden and crispy, turning the wings every 5 minutes to make sure they brown evenly. Brush occasionally with some of the remaining marinade, but not in the last 5 minutes of cooking time.

The first run, like first love, is always the best, always the fullest, always the sweetest.

— John Burroughs, *Winter Sunshine*

Lemon-Basil Salad Dressing

SOMEBODY COULD BOTTLE this and make a fortune, that's how good it is. And it's very versatile. I use it on green salads, three-bean salads, and Green Bean Salad (page 72).

Ingredients

- ⅓ cup vegetable oil or part vegetable oil and part olive oil
- ¼ cup apple cider vinegar
- ¼ cup pure maple syrup
- 1 tablespoon Dijon mustard
- 1½ teaspoons minced fresh basil or ½ teaspoon crushed dried basil
- ⅛ teaspoon finely grated lemon zest
- Salt and freshly ground black pepper

1 Whisk together the oil, vinegar, maple syrup, mustard, basil, lemon zest, and salt and pepper to taste in a small bowl.

2 Taste, and adjust the flavor with a little more maple or vinegar, if needed. Transfer to a bottle and refrigerate.

VARIATION To make a creamy version, prepare the dressing as above. Whisk in ½ to ¾ cup sour cream.

Salads & Sauces

BEYOND BREAKFAST

71

Green Bean Salad

COOL, CRISP, AND COLORFUL, this is likely to become one of your most requested summer salads. It is best if the salad is left for at least an hour in the refrigerator before it is served.

Ingredients

      Salt
  3 cups fresh green beans, ends trimmed, halved
  ½ cup Lemon-Basil Salad Dressing (page 71)
  1 small red onion, halved and thinly sliced
  ½ cup finely chopped red bell pepper
  1 stalk celery, finely chopped
  1 tablespoon capers, optional but highly recommended
      Freshly ground black pepper

1 Bring 2 quarts of salted water to a boil in a large pot. Add the beans and boil them until just tender, 6 to 8 minutes. Drain and transfer to a large bowl.

2 Immediately stir in the dressing, onion, bell pepper, celery, capers, if desired, and salt and pepper to taste. Let cool thoroughly. Cover and refrigerate for at least 1 hour before serving.

Jícama, Grape, and Orange Salad

YIELD: 4–5 servings

JÍCAMA (HEE-KAH-MAH) is one of those vegetables I'd never heard of when growing up. It looks something like a flattened potato, comes in a whole range of sizes, and is imported from Mexico. It's a bit plain, but adaptable, and it perks up in raw salads of this sort. Do let the salad sit in the refrigerator for a couple of hours before serving; bathing in the acid juices really helps the character of the jícama.

Ingredients

- 1 small jícama
  Juice of 2 medium limes (about 3 tablespoons)
- 2½ tablespoons pure maple syrup
- 1 tablespoon vegetable oil
  Pinch of salt
- 1 orange
- ½ cup seedless green grapes, halved
- 2 tablespoons minced red onion

1 Peel the jícama with a paring knife and cut lengthwise into ¼-inch slabs. Cut the slabs into ¼-inch-wide strips, then gather the strips and slice them into ¼-inch cubes. Put 1½ to 2 cups in a medium bowl.

2 Pour the lime juice, maple syrup, and oil over the jícama; toss. Stir in the salt.

3 Halve the orange, remove any seeds, then free the sections with a knife. Squeeze them and their juices into the bowl, then add the grapes and onion. Cover and refrigerate for several hours before serving; stir once or twice while it's chilling.

*The scarlet of the maples can shake me like a cry
Of bugles going by.*

— William Bliss Carman

Cucumber-Apple Raita

YIELD: 4–6 servings

THIS YOGURT-BASED Indian dish is a cool, refreshing counterpoint to spicy curries, though it could be served with any number of savory foods. There's an agreeable balance of sweet and sharp flavors, with the maple sounding a soft background note. A pinch of chopped fresh mint really makes this shine, if you happen to have some on hand.

Ingredients

- 1 large cucumber, peeled, halved, and seeded
- ¼ teaspoon salt
- 1¼ cups plain yogurt
- 1½ tablespoons pure maple syrup
- 1 tablespoon minced onion
- ½ teaspoon finely grated orange zest
- 1 tart, firm apple, peeled, cored, and quartered

1 Chop the cucumber into small uniform dice and transfer to a small bowl. Stir in the salt and set aside for 30 minutes.

2 Stir together the yogurt, maple syrup, onion, and orange zest. Chop the apple into small uniform dice and stir into the yogurt. Cover and refrigerate for 30 minutes.

3 Squeeze the excess moisture out of the cucumber with your hands and fold the cucumbers into the yogurt mixture. Chill for at least 1 hour more, preferably longer, before serving.

Roasted Pepper and Chickpea Salad

THE FLAVORS OF THIS SALAD create the nicest harmony. Do use smoked cheddar — it combines nicely with the maple. Serve with grilled foods.

Ingredients

Dressing

- ¼ cup vegetable oil
- Juice of 1 medium lemon (about 2 tablespoons)
- 2 tablespoons pure maple syrup
- 1½ tablespoons Dijon mustard

Salad

- 3 large green or red bell peppers
- 2 cups cooked chickpeas (about 1 cup dried; rinsed and drained if using canned)
- 2 tablespoons minced onion
- ½ cup diced smoked cheddar cheese
- ½ cup diced prosciutto or ham
- Salt and freshly ground black pepper

1 FOR THE DRESSING: Whisk together the oil, lemon juice, maple syrup, and mustard in a large salad bowl. Set aside.

2 FOR THE SALAD: Roast the whole peppers on a grill, over a hot burner, or under a broiler, turning often with tongs, until the entire surface is charred. Put the peppers into a plastic bag, twist shut, and freeze for 15 minutes — this will steam off the skins. Cut out the stem ends, drain, and halve them. Remove the seeds and skins; the skins should peel off readily. Slice the peppers into narrow strips.

3 Toss the peppers into the dressing along with the chickpeas, onion, cheese, and prosciutto. Stir. Chill for several hours. Season to taste with salt and pepper before serving.

The Roasting Difference

There was a time when I wouldn't bother with roasting peppers. When I actually did try it, though, I was amazed at what a difference the roasting made in flavor and texture. In summer, I like to roast peppers on a hot grill; in other seasons, on top of the burner grid on my gas stove. You can also broil peppers in a shallow pan in any oven. For detailed instructions, see step 2 of this recipe.

Thai-Inspired Mushroom Salad

YIELD: 6 servings

DON'T LET the longish list of ingredients deter you: The need for the mushrooms to marinate in the refrigerator makes this a perfect do-ahead dish. And your taste buds will thank you.

Ingredients

- ¾ pound white mushrooms
- ½ pound shiitake mushrooms
- ½ cup rice vinegar
- ¼ cup orange juice
- 3 tablespoons pure maple syrup
- 3 tablespoons olive oil
- 2 tablespoons peanut butter
- 2 tablespoons tamari or soy sauce
- 1 tablespoon toasted sesame oil
- ¼ teaspoon hot sauce (a mango-flavored one is nice)
- 3 scallions (2 optional)
- 1 clove garlic, crushed
- 1 teaspoon grated fresh gingerroot
- 1 teaspoon finely minced lemongrass or lemon zest
- 6 cups (8 ounces) mesclun or baby spinach
- ½ medium red bell pepper, diced, optional

1 Trim and slice the white mushrooms and put them in a large nonreactive bowl. Remove and discard the shiitake stems and slice the caps; add them to the bowl. Set aside.

2 Whisk together the vinegar, orange juice, maple syrup, olive oil, peanut butter, tamari, sesame oil, and hot sauce in a medium saucepan.

3 Finely mince one of the scallions; add to the vinegar mixture. Stir in the garlic, gingerroot, and lemongrass.

4 Cook the mixture, stirring constantly, over low heat until it just comes to a simmer, about 5 minutes. Pour over the mushrooms; toss to coat. Cover and refrigerate for at least 3 hours or up to 3 days.

5 Divide the mesclun among six salad plates. Drain the mushrooms, then spoon them on top of the mesclun. Scatter the red pepper on the mushrooms, if desired. Slice the remaining two scallions diagonally into ½-inch pieces, if desired, and top the red pepper with them. Serve immediately.

Creamy Maple Syrup Dressing

YIELD: About 1½ cups

THIS IS A GREAT RECIPE for something special at the last minute, because the ingredients for this dressing are kitchen staples in most homes. Created by the Ontario Maple Syrup Producers Association, it's just the right touch over butter lettuce or sliced fruit or berries.

Ingredients

- 1 cup mayonnaise
- ½ cup pure maple syrup
- ¼ cup apple cider vinegar

1 Whisk together the mayonnaise, maple syrup, and vinegar in a small bowl until smooth.

2 Refrigerate, tightly covered, for at least 1 hour to let the flavors blend.

Salad Oils

When making salad dressings, I call for vegetable oil and sometimes suggest that part olive oil is okay. Here's a place where your personal taste preferences come into play. Some people use only olive oil in salad dressings, but a good-quality extra-virgin olive oil with lots of fruity flavor can overpower other ingredients in a dressing, particularly a light maple syrup. Canola, corn, peanut, safflower, soy, and sunflower oils are mild enough to let other flavors shine through.

Maple Syrup Production Statistics

With improved technology and increased demand for maple syrup and its related products, maple syrup production has grown dramatically during the past decade.

Sugarmaker and producer associations contribute both to the research efforts, by making grants to researchers, and to the increased demand, through concerted and coordinated marketing efforts.

While Vermont maintains its place as the largest U.S. producer, Quebec is now the world leader. See below how the states and provinces stacked up in 2013.

STATE/PROVINCE	GALLONS
Quebec	9,083,000
Vermont	1,480,000
New York	574,000
Maine	560,000
New Brunswick	484,000
Ontario	449,000
Wisconsin	265,000
Ohio	155,000
Michigan	148,000
Pennsylvania	134,000
New Hampshire	124,000
Massachusetts	63,000
Connecticut	20,000

Maple Balsamic Dressing

JANICE WENTWORTH of the Warren Farm & Sugarhouse in North Brookfield, Massachusetts, adapted this recipe from *Sweet Maple: Life, Lore & Recipes from the Sugarbush,* which was copublished in 1993 by *Vermont Life* magazine and Chapters Publishing. The lime juice and cilantro give it the Southwestern flair that Jan's family loves. This dressing brings out the fruit flavor in any green salad with fruit in it.

Ingredients

- 3 tablespoons balsamic vinegar
- 2 tablespoons pure maple syrup
  Juice of 1 lime (about 1 tablespoon)
- 1 clove garlic, minced
- 1 teaspoon finely chopped fresh cilantro
- 1 teaspoon dry mustard
- 1 cup extra-virgin olive oil
  Salt and freshly ground black pepper

1 Combine the vinegar, maple syrup, lime juice, garlic, cilantro, and mustard in a food processor or blender.

2 With the motor running, slowly pour the oil in through the feed tube until the dressing is emulsified. Add salt and pepper to taste.

3 Transfer to a bottle and refrigerate. The dressing may be stored for several weeks. Shake well before using.

Maple sugaring will not be hurried. It is more than the work of one night or one week; its rhythms are measured in sunlight and shadow, in the tilt of the earth's axis and in the ancient memories of trees.

— Will Weaver, from the foreword to *Sugartime* by Susan Carol Hauser

Salads & Sauces

BEYOND BREAKFAST

Spicy Sweet-and-Sour Dressing

YIELD: About 1 cup

JUST A LITTLE BIT of this goes a long way to brighten up a tossed salad with an Asian accent. And this is the dressing of choice for the Sweet-and-Sour Chicken-Cashew Salad (page 107).

Ingredients

- ¼ cup vegetable oil (part vegetable oil and part olive oil is good, too)
- ¼ cup apple cider vinegar
- ¼ cup pure maple syrup
- 3 tablespoons tamari or soy sauce
- 1 tablespoon Dijon mustard
- 1 clove garlic, minced
- ¼ teaspoon finely grated orange zest
- ⅛ teaspoon cayenne pepper
- ⅛ teaspoon ground cinnamon
- ⅛ teaspoon ground cloves
- ⅛ teaspoon ground ginger

1 Combine the oil, vinegar, maple syrup, tamari, mustard, garlic, orange zest, cayenne, cinnamon, cloves, and ginger in a small bowl and whisk thoroughly. Taste and correct the precise balance of ingredients to your liking, adding a bit more vinegar, maple syrup, or spice, if you like.

2 Transfer to a bottle and refrigerate. Shake well before using.

North Country Basting Sauce

YIELD: About 3 cups

THOUGH NOT FAITHFUL to any particular school of thought on barbecue sauce, I can tell you that this barbecue sauce is versatile, spicy, and no slouch in the flavor department. It's tops on barbecued or broiled chicken. One thing I like to do with it is to combine it with hot peppers, more spices, and onions, for the Hot and Spicy Shrimp and Sausage Kabobs (page 108).

Ingredients

1 cup ketchup
⅔ cup apple cider vinegar
½ cup vegetable oil
½ cup pure maple syrup
1 tablespoon Worcestershire sauce
1 tablespoon Dijon mustard
½ teaspoon chili powder
½ teaspoon salt
¼ teaspoon cayenne pepper

1 Bring the ketchup, vinegar, oil, maple syrup, Worcestershire, mustard, chili powder, salt, and cayenne to a boil in a small saucepan over medium heat, stirring occasionally. Decrease the heat and cook gently for 10 minutes, stirring from time to time.

2 Let cool, then store in a covered jar in the refrigerator, where it will keep for at least 4 weeks.

Maple History

Legend in the United States has designated the first maple syrup maker and cook as an Iroquois woman, the wife of one Chief Woksis. One late-winter morning, the story goes, the chief headed out on one of his hunts, but not before yanking his tomahawk from the tree where he'd thrown it the night before. On this particular day the weather turned quite warm, causing the tree's sap to run and fill a container standing near the trunk. The woman spied the vessel and, thinking it was plain water, cooked her evening meal in it. The boiling that ensued turned the sap to syrup, flavoring the chief's meal as never before. And thus began the tradition of making maple syrup.

Maple-Mustard Barbecue Sauce

YIELD: ¾ cup

SIMPLE AND YUMMY, this recipe makes enough for one chicken or pork tenderloin, or one batch of burgers — pass the barbecue sauce instead of ketchup. It was devised by the Maine Maple Producers Association to inspire people to use maple syrup at meals other than breakfast.

Ingredients

- ⅓ cup pure maple syrup
- 2 tablespoons Dijon mustard or other strong mustard
  Juice of 1 medium lemon (about 2 tablespoons)
- 1 clove garlic, crushed
- 1 teaspoon cracked black pepper
- ½ teaspoon dried thyme, crushed
- ⅓ cup peanut or other mild oil

1 Whisk together the maple syrup, mustard, lemon juice, garlic, pepper, and thyme in a medium bowl.

2 Slowly whisk in the oil to emulsify the sauce. Refrigerate, tightly covered, for up to several weeks.

Basting Safety

Don't reuse marinade or sauce used on raw meat, poultry, or seafood unless you boil it first to destroy any bacteria. If you're brushing sauce on food while it's grilling, don't do so during the last 5 minutes of cooking time. These food safety practices are recommended by the U.S. Department of Agriculture.

Maple-Basil Mustard

NOT TO BLOW MY OWN HORN, but my friend Dan says that his father — who collects mustards from all over the world — says this rivals the best of them. I know I sure like it, and I bet you will, too. It has guts, but with a pleasant, grainy personality. I use it on sandwiches and in salad dressings and marinades — with just about anything that calls for mustard.

Ingredients

- ⅓ cup yellow mustard seeds
- 2 tablespoons dry mustard (I like Colman's)
- ½ cup water
- ⅓ cup apple cider vinegar
- ⅓ cup pure maple syrup
- ¾ teaspoon salt
- 1 teaspoon dried basil

---

1 Put the mustard seeds, dry mustard, and water in a food processor or blender and process for 30 to 60 seconds, until the mixture takes on a thick, grainy texture. Scrape into a bowl and let sit, uncovered, for 2 hours or more; this helps release some of the bitter components.

2 After several hours, return the mixture to the food processor. Add the vinegar, maple syrup, salt, and basil and process until slightly smooth yet still somewhat grainy.

3 Scrape into the top of a double boiler and cook over simmering water for about 10 minutes, stirring often. Scrape into a bowl and let cool. Taste. It may need a touch more maple or salt or vinegar. Pack into a jar with a lid, then refrigerate; it will keep indefinitely.

Beet and Pear Relish

YOU CAN DO ALL SORTS of things with this sweet relish. In summer I like to serve it as is, on a plate with a variety of cold nibbles (try stirring in some chopped fresh mint). In the cooler months, I gently cook the whole shebang in a saucepan with a large handful of cranberries, until the cranberries pop and soften — maybe 10 minutes. This I serve with poultry or pork. Depending on how many cranberries you use, it might need a touch more maple to round off the tart edge. This keeps well in the refrigerator in a tightly covered jar.

Ingredients

- 4 medium beets
- 1 firm, ripe pear, peeled, cored, and diced
- ⅓ cup chopped raisins
- 3 tablespoons pure maple syrup
- Juice of 1 lemon (about 2 tablespoons)
- 1 teaspoon minced fresh gingerroot or ¼ teaspoon ground ginger
- ⅛ teaspoon ground cinnamon

1 Put the beets in a saucepan and add cold water to cover. Bring to a boil, then decrease the heat, cover the pan, and simmer until tender, about 30 minutes. Check for doneness by removing a beet and squeezing it quickly with your fingers; the beet will yield to the pressure when done. Drain the beets and run them under cold water.

2 When the beets are cool enough to handle, rub off the skins. Cut the beets into small dice.

3 Combine the beets, pear, raisins, maple syrup, lemon juice, gingerroot, and cinnamon in a medium bowl. Stir well. Refrigerate, covered, until ready to serve.

Braised Onions with Bacon

YIELD: 4–5 servings

I'VE REALLY TRIED to like whole onions in the past but never really cared for any of the recipes I found. Until this one. This is nothing less than a sensational way to prepare boiled onions to serve with roasts, steak, and other meats. What you do is briefly sauté the onions in bacon fat, add water and seasonings, then cover and braise. Then you finish them with a touch of maple syrup and sprinkle on the bacon. Better to choose the medium boiling onions than the tiny ones; it saves work in peeling.

Ingredients

- 1 pound medium boiling onions
- 3 slices bacon
- ½ cup water
- 1 teaspoon soy sauce
- 1 bay leaf
- ¼ teaspoon dried thyme
- 2 tablespoons pure maple syrup

---

1 Peel the onions and cut off the hairy part at the root end. Make a small shallow X in the root end, to encourage even cooking.

2 Sauté the bacon until crisp in a heavy skillet. Using a slotted spoon or spatula, remove the bacon, blot with paper towels, and set aside. Add the onions to the fat and stir to coat. Cook over medium heat, partially covered, for 5 minutes, stirring occasionally.

3 Stir in the water, soy sauce, bay leaf, and thyme. Cover, decrease the heat slightly, and braise until the onions are almost tender all the way through, 10 to 15 minutes. The exact cooking time will depend on the size of the onions.

4 Stir the maple syrup into the pan — which will still have a thin layer of liquid in it — and turn up the heat. Cook and stir until the liquid turns to a syrupy glaze; it shouldn't take long. Crumble the bacon and stir it in. Remove the bay leaf. Serve hot, spooning on any available glaze.

VARIATION You can make this a vegetarian dish by sautéing the onions in olive oil instead of bacon fat. Garnish with seasoned croutons.

Pineapple Salsa

LIGHT AND FRUITY, this salsa makes a great topping for grilled fish, chicken, or pork. Or dollop it on fresh greens for a tasty salad.

Ingredients
- 1 cup finely chopped fresh pineapple
- 2 tablespoons finely minced red onion or scallion
- 1 tablespoon chopped fresh cilantro or mint
- 1 serrano chile, seeded and finely minced
- Juice of 1 small lime (about 1 tablespoon)
- 1 tablespoon pure maple syrup

1 Combine the pineapple, onion, cilantro, chile, lime juice, and maple syrup in a medium bowl.

2 Refrigerate, covered, for at least 1 hour or up to 2 days before serving.

Maple Baked Beans

BAKED BEANS, LIKE CHILI, is one of those dishes that ignites controversy. Almost every variable can be debated. At the risk of adding fuel to the fire, here is my own favorite maple version.

Boston Baked Beans

The mixture of beans, salt pork, molasses, and brown sugar popularly called Boston baked beans is said to be named after the tradition of Boston's Puritan women, who often prepared the dish for Saturday's supper, then served leftovers for breakfast the next morning because cooking on the Sabbath was forbidden. To make the meal authentic, add Steamed Brown Bread (page 95).

Ingredients

- 1 pound dried navy or pea beans
- ⅓ cup vegetable oil
- 1 cup chopped onion
- 1 green bell pepper, chopped
- 1 stalk celery, chopped
- 2–3 cloves garlic, minced
- ½ cup pure maple syrup
- ½ cup tomato purée or crushed tomatoes
- 2 tablespoons blackstrap molasses
- 2 tablespoons apple cider vinegar
- 1 tablespoon Dijon mustard
- ¼ cup chopped fresh flat-leaf parsley
- 1 bay leaf
- 1½ teaspoons salt
- ¼ teaspoon freshly ground black pepper

1 Pick the beans over, removing any rubble such as sticks and pebbles. Rinse them well, then place in a large bowl with plenty of hot water. Let soak for at least 1 hour, or as long as overnight. Drain, then combine the beans with about 4 quarts fresh water in a large pot. Bring to a boil, and then decrease the heat. Simmer, partially covered, just until tender, 1½ to 2 hours. Drain the beans, reserving the cooking water, and put the beans into a large bowl.

2 While the beans cook, heat the oil in a large skillet. Add the onion, pepper, and celery, and sauté for several minutes, adding the garlic at the end. Remove from the heat. Set aside. Preheat the oven to 325°F/170°C.

3 Whisk together 1 cup of the reserved cooking water, the maple syrup, tomato purée, molasses, vinegar, mustard, parsley, bay leaf, salt, and pepper in a medium bowl.

4 Add the sautéed vegetables and the maple mixture to the beans; mix well. Pour the beans into a large shallow casserole dish and cover tightly. Bake until the beans are soft and cloaked in a thick, saucy glaze, 2½ to 3½ hours. Check periodically to make sure they have enough liquid, adding more of the reserved cooking water, if necessary.

Maple Bread-and-Butter Pickles

THESE REFRIGERATOR PICKLES are a cinch to prepare and require no special equipment beyond clean jars to pack them in. (I like half-pint jars because I'm left with a couple of jars to give away with each batch.) Refrigerator pickles get better with age and will keep for at least 6 to 8 weeks in the fridge.

Ingredients
- 2 pounds small pickling cucumbers (such as Kirby)
- 1 medium sweet onion, halved and thinly sliced
- 1½ tablespoons kosher salt
- 1¼ cups apple cider vinegar
- 1 cup sugar
- ½ cup pure maple syrup
- ¼ cup water
- 1 tablespoon yellow mustard seeds
- 1 teaspoon celery seeds
- ¼ teaspoon red pepper flakes

1 Thoroughly wash six half-pint canning jars in hot water; jelly or condiment jars will also work. Dry well and set aside.

2 Slice the cucumbers — on the bias for larger slices — a hair less than ¼ inch thick. Transfer the slices to a large bowl and add the onion. Sprinkle with the salt and mix well, by hand, making sure the salt is well distributed. Cover with plastic wrap and set aside for 2 hours at room temperature.

3 When the 2 hours have elapsed, combine the vinegar, sugar, maple syrup, water, mustard seeds, celery seeds, and red pepper in a large saucepan. Bring to a simmer, stirring, then simmer gently for 5 minutes, making sure the sugar has dissolved.

4 Drain the cucumbers in a colander, then rinse briefly under cold water and drain again. Divide the cucumber slices and onions evenly among the jars, packing them tightly. Add enough of the hot brine mixture to each jar to cover the slices. (I transfer the brine to a spouted bowl for easy pouring.) Slide a knife down the edge to remove any air pockets. Screw on the lids, allow the jars to cool, then refrigerate. Allow the pickles to marinate in the fridge for at least 24 hours before serving.

Vegetables & Sides

Stuffed Sweet Potatoes

YIELD: 4 servings

HERE'S AN EASY, fun recipe, and a nice switch from candied sweet potatoes. I stuff only the best shells because I like the potatoes to be extra full.

Ingredients

- 4 medium sweet potatoes (about 2½ pounds)
- ¼ cup pure maple syrup
- ¼ cup sour cream
- 1 tablespoon butter
- ¼ teaspoon salt
- Pinch of ground cinnamon
- Pinch of ground nutmeg
- Pinch of ground cloves
- Brown sugar for sprinkling, optional

1 Preheat the oven to 400°F/200°C. Prick the potatoes with a fork, once each, and bake on a baking sheet for 50 to 60 minutes, until the insides are soft. Remove from the oven and set aside until they are cool enough to handle.

2 Halve the potatoes lengthwise, carefully scoop out the insides, and reserve the shells. Combine the insides in a large bowl with the maple syrup, sour cream, butter, salt, cinnamon, nutmeg, and cloves. Whip with an electric mixer until smooth. Pack the four best shells with the filling, mounding it in. Place close together in a pie plate or small casserole dish. Sprinkle the tops with a touch of brown sugar, if desired. Bake for 20 to 25 minutes, until heated through.

Ne-naw-Bozhoo or Manabush?

Native American legend has it that Ne-naw-Bozhoo added the water in maple sap, but in Canada the legend of Nokomis (Earth) attributes that act to another. The Canadian story relates that Nokomis was the first to harvest syrup from the maple tree. It's said that Nokomis's grandson Manabush did not want people to become lazy by enjoying maple syrup without working for it, so he emptied a large vessel of water into the maple tree to dilute the syrup. Since then, people have had to boil the sap to obtain the trees' sugar.

Tom McCrumm

TOM MᴄCRUMM was not born to sugar making; he was called to it. It's become his profession and his passion. And he revels in sharing it.

When Tom was growing up, his family visited the Adirondacks, where they bought maple syrup at a farm. With eyes sparkling, he describes his lifelong fascination with a process where "you can take something that looks like water out of a tree and make something so good."

Later, he visited friends who boiled their own syrup, and while living on the West Virginia–Virginia border he made a gallon or two on his own. The mystery of sugaring brought him to Cornell University's maple research facility. Eventually, he bought South Face Farm in Ashfield, Massachusetts, where he collects sap from 4,000 to 4,500 taps. He also grows and sells Christmas trees, all the while keeping his year-round maple mail-order business going.

Tom runs a restaurant at his sugarhouse on weekends during sugaring season; his wife, Judy Haupt, bakes the pies for the sugarhouse. The days often start at 5:30 A.M. and end toward midnight during the season, but Tom wouldn't have it any other way. At the sugarhouse, people waiting to get their fill of pancakes watch Tom boiling sap and ask questions. He says he "wants people to leave with a full brain and a full stomach," and so he talks about the science of production, such as indicators for the precise moment when the sap has become syrup and the right temperature and density to watch for so that the syrup won't burn. And then he discusses the art: "You'll be boiling and, just like that, you see in one spot by the way it's boiling and the steam is rolling off that it's about to burn. You gain a feel for it." Tom's eyes are sparkling again. (His favorite recipe for Maple-Glazed Butternut Squash is on page 99.)

Maple-Roasted Root Vegetables

YIELD: 4 servings

OVEN ROASTING seems to bring out the best in vegetables, especially these winter roots. The slow cooking in a mapley sauce fills the kitchen with mouthwatering aromas and produces one of my favorite down-home comfort foods.

Ingredients

- 3 medium carrots, peeled and cut into 1¼-inch chunks
- 3 medium parsnips, peeled and cut into 1¼-inch chunks
- 1 small yellow turnip (about ½ pound), peeled and cut into 1¼-inch chunks
- ½ cup pure maple syrup
- 4 tablespoons butter
- ¼ cup bourbon or rum
- 1½ teaspoons salt
- Freshly ground black pepper

---

1 Preheat the oven to 350°F/180°C. Arrange the carrots, parsnips, and turnip in a single layer in a shallow roasting pan.

2 Heat the maple syrup and butter in a small saucepan just until the butter is melted, about 2 minutes. Remove from the heat. Stir in the bourbon.

3 Pour the maple mixture over the vegetables and toss to thoroughly coat. Sprinkle the vegetables with the salt and pepper to taste.

4 Cover the pan with aluminum foil and bake for 25 minutes. Remove the pan from the oven, stir the vegetables, and bake, uncovered, 20 to 25 minutes longer, until tender.

Steamed Brown Bread

YIELD: 2 round loaves, 8–10 slices each

TRADITIONALLY this bread is made with molasses, not maple syrup, but once you've tasted this version, I think you'll excuse the liberties I've taken. Some folks don't like to tamper with tradition. I can remember publishing a recipe for Boston brown bread in a magazine, only to have some irate fellow write to the editor, blasting me for instructing readers to cut this with a sharp, serrated knife. Of course, the only correct way to slice it, this fellow maintained, was with twine — you wrap it around the loaf and pull the ends. Whether you use a knife, twine, or dental floss to slice it, do serve it with softened cream cheese. Some people like to soak the raisins in a little rum beforehand.

Ingredients

- 1 cup cornmeal
- 1 cup rye flour
- 1 cup whole-wheat flour
- 1 teaspoon baking powder
- 1 teaspoon baking soda
- 1 teaspoon salt
- 2 cups buttermilk
- 1 cup pure maple syrup
- 1 cup raisins

---

1 Grease two 13- or 16-ounce coffee cans, including the insides of their plastic lids. Place a trivet, large enough to support both cans, in the bottom of a wide, deep pot. Add hot water to about 3 inches above the trivet. Place the pot on a burner over medium heat.

2 Toss the cornmeal, flours, baking powder, baking soda, and salt to mix in a large bowl. In a separate bowl, beat the buttermilk and maple syrup.

3 Make a well in the dry ingredients, add the buttermilk mixture, and stir just to blend. Fold in the raisins.

4 Divide the batter evenly between the cans and put on the lids. Wrap a large piece of aluminum foil over each lid and secure with a heavy rubber band or twine. Using a paring knife, poke a couple of steam vents in the foil. Put the cans in the water; the level should rise one-half to two-thirds of the way up the sides of the cans. Cover the pot with its lid if it will fit, or fashion a foil tent.

5 Bring the water to a boil. Decrease the heat and simmer for approximately 2 hours. Check the water level once or twice, and replenish with boiling water if it falls below the halfway mark. The bread is done when a tester inserted deeply into the center emerges clean. Remove the bread from the cans.

6 Preheat the oven to 350°F/180°C. Lightly grease a baking sheet. Place the breads on the prepared baking sheet and bake for 5 minutes to dry the outside surfaces. Serve warm, or transfer the bread to a wire rack to cool completely.

Vegetables & Sides

BEYOND BREAKFAST

Sweet Corn and Butternut Squash Succotash

YIELD: 4–5 servings

WHAT THIS SUCCOTASH lacks in tradition (no lima beans) it more than makes up for with great flavor and eye appeal. Sweetened with a touch of maple syrup, it's a welcome side dish with just about any meat, from robust pork barbecue to sautéed chicken breasts. I'll often garnish the succotash with crumbles of feta cheese, the saltiness of the cheese being the perfect counterpoint to the delicate maple syrup.

Ingredients

- 2 tablespoons butter
- ½ large onion, finely chopped
- 2 cups peeled, seeded, and diced butternut squash (¼-inch pieces)
- 2 cups fresh or frozen corn kernels, thawed if frozen (at least partially)
- ¼ teaspoon smoked paprika or paprika
- ¾ cup chicken broth
- 1 teaspoon Dijon mustard
  Salt and freshly ground black pepper
- 1½ tablespoons pure maple syrup
  Crumbled feta cheese for serving, optional

1 Melt the butter in a large skillet over medium heat. Add the onion and sauté for 2 to 3 minutes. Stir in the squash, corn, and paprika. Cook the vegetables for 2 to 3 minutes, stirring often. Stir in the chicken broth and mustard, and add salt and pepper to taste.

2 Cover the dish and braise the vegetables until the squash is barely tender, 6 to 7 minutes. Uncover the skillet and continue to cook until virtually all of the liquid has cooked off; this should take only a couple of minutes. Stir in the maple syrup. Cook for another minute, stirring pretty much nonstop so everything is evenly coated. Taste again, adding more salt and pepper, if desired.

3 Transfer the succotash to a serving dish and serve immediately. If you're using the cheese, put it in a small bowl and pass it at the table.

Whole-Wheat and Oat Yeast Loaves or Rolls

IT TAKES A CONSIDERABLE AMOUNT of maple syrup to get any kind of clear maple flavor from a yeast bread. I do have a trick, however, for accenting the maple flavor when I use this recipe to make rolls, as I often do. What I do is brush the rolls after they have risen with a mixture of 1 tablespoon melted butter and 1 tablespoon maple syrup, which not only clarifies the maple flavor but also gives the baked rolls a dark, glossy sheen. Don't do this on the loaves, however, because the tops will burn during the longer baking time. This makes an excellent toasting loaf.

Ingredients

Vegetable oil for the bowl
1¼ cups milk
¾ cup buttermilk
¾ cup old-fashioned rolled oats
⅓ cup warm water (105–115°F/40–45°C)
1 tablespoon active dry yeast
3½ cups whole-wheat flour
5 tablespoons butter, softened
⅔ cup pure maple syrup
1 egg, lightly beaten
1 tablespoon salt
3 cups unbleached all-purpose flour

1 Lightly oil a large bowl. Set aside.

2 Warm the milk and buttermilk in a saucepan until hot to the touch. Put the oats in a large bowl and pour the warm milk over them.

3 Pour the water into a separate small bowl and sprinkle on the yeast. When the oat liquid cools to about body temperature, stir in the dissolved yeast. Using a heavy wooden spoon, stir 2 cups of the whole-wheat flour into the liquid, beating hard for 1 minute. Cover this "sponge" and let rise for 1 hour.

4 Beat the softened butter into the sponge, followed by the maple syrup, egg, and salt. Stir in the remaining 1½ cups whole-wheat flour. Cover and let rise for 10 minutes.

5 Now start stirring in the all-purpose flour, about ½ cup at a time, until the dough becomes too stiff to beat (you may use slightly more or less than 3 cups). Turn the dough onto a floured surface. Begin kneading, gently at first, using more flour as needed to prevent sticking. Knead for a good 10 minutes, or until the dough is smooth and fairly elastic. Place in the oiled bowl and turn to coat the entire surface. Cover and let rise until double in bulk, about 1 hour.

6 Grease two large loaf pans. Punch the dough down, knead briefly, and divide it in half. Shape the dough into loaves and place the loaves in the prepared pans. (I like to roll it out into a tapered rectangle, with the taper toward me, and roll up the dough like a carpet; this puts adequate tension on the dough and gives the top a nice, rounded appearance.)

7 Cover and let double in bulk, 30 to 45 minutes. Preheat the oven to 375°F/190°C when the loaves are almost doubled.

8 When fully doubled, bake the loaves for about 45 minutes, or until nicely browned. Remove the loaves from their pans and let cool on a rack. Store in plastic bags.

Note: To make dinner rolls, follow the directions for steps 1–5, then break off golf ball–size pieces of dough and shape into rounds. Place, almost touching, on a greased baking sheet. Let rise, brush with glaze (see recipe introduction), and bake for 25 to 30 minutes.

Maple-Glazed Butternut Squash

YIELD: 4 servings

TOM McCRUMM of South Face Farm in Ashfield, Massachusetts, and former executive director of the Massachusetts Maple Producers Association, says he is not a fan of butternut squash. Unless, of course, it's glazed with maple syrup seasoned by the subtle nutmeg flavor of mace, as in this recipe created by Tom's wife, Judy Haupt.

Ingredients

- 1 medium butternut squash (about 1½ pounds)
- ⅔ cup water
- ¼ cup pure maple syrup
- ¼ cup dark rum
- ¼ teaspoon ground mace

1 Peel, seed, and quarter the squash. Cut crosswise into ½-inch slices to make about 5½ cups.

2 Bring the squash, water, maple syrup, rum, and mace to a boil in a large saucepan over medium-high heat. Decrease the heat and simmer, covered, until the squash is tender, about 15 minutes. While the squash is simmering, warm a serving dish in a 200°F/90°C oven or by filling it with very hot water.

3 Transfer the squash with a slotted spoon to the warmed serving dish; reserve the cooking liquid.

4 Increase the heat and boil the cooking liquid until it is thickened, about 3 minutes. Pour the thickened liquid over the squash.

Maple-Glazed Brussels Sprouts

BRUSSELS SPROUTS have a special affinity for maple syrup, and it gets even better when you dress them up with bacon. Serve them at the holidays or anytime you cook a roast. These are so delicious that I've seen these open the most steadfastly closed Brussels sprouts minds.

Ingredients

- 4 slices bacon
- 1 tablespoon butter
- 1 cup finely chopped sweet onion
- 1–1¼ pounds Brussels sprouts, halved
- ½ cup chicken broth
- 1 tablespoon Dijon mustard
- Salt and freshly ground black pepper
- 2 tablespoons pure maple syrup

1 Cook the bacon in a large skillet until crisp. Transfer the bacon to paper towels and let cool. Tilt the skillet and spoon off all but about 2 tablespoons of the fat.

2 Add the butter and onions to the skillet. Sauté the onions over medium heat until translucent, 7 to 8 minutes. Stir in the Brussels sprouts and cook for 2 minutes, stirring occasionally. Stir in the chicken broth.

3 Cover and braise the Brussels sprouts until not quite tender, about 3 minutes. Uncover the pan, stir in the mustard, and add salt and pepper to taste. Continue to cook, uncovered, until the Brussels sprouts are tender and the liquid is reduced to a glaze, 2 to 3 minutes. Stir in the maple syrup just before taking them off the heat. Transfer to a serving plate and crumble the bacon over the top. Serve immediately.

Meatloaf with Ham

YIELD: 8 or more servings

MOVE OVER, plain old meatloaf — you've got some serious competition with this savory, maple-infused main dish. Serve it with the usual trimmings, like mashed potatoes and your favorite steamed greens. Ground ham isn't something that's easy to find in most markets, so you can grind your own in a food grinder from chunks of leftover ham. Or use the food processor, starting with well-diced ham. Pulse the machine just until it's finely chopped; you don't want it to turn smooth or gummy.

Ingredients

Butter for greasing
1½ pounds ground pork
1½ pounds ground ham
½ cup quick-cooking rolled oats
½ cup fine cracker crumbs or plain dry bread crumbs
1 cup finely chopped onion
2 tablespoons finely chopped fresh flat-leaf parsley
½ teaspoon (scant) salt
1 teaspoon dry mustard
½ teaspoon smoked paprika
¼ teaspoon ground allspice
¼ teaspoon freshly ground black pepper
⅛ teaspoon cayenne pepper
2 eggs
¾ cup milk
1 teaspoon yellow mustard

Glaze

⅓ cup pure maple syrup
⅓ cup firmly packed brown sugar
2 tablespoons apple cider vinegar
1½ tablespoons Dijon mustard
1 teaspoon Worcestershire sauce

1 Preheat the oven to 350°F/180°C. Lightly butter a very large loaf pan, one that's at least 5 by 9 inches. (You many need one or two ramekins for the extra loaf mixture since this makes a lot, so get those out, too, just in case.)

2 Combine the pork, ham, oats, cracker crumbs, onion, and parsley in a very large bowl. Using your hands, break up the meats, rubbing with the crumbs until everything is good and mixed. Sprinkle on the salt, dry mustard, paprika, allspice, black pepper, and cayenne; mix again.

3 Whisk the eggs, milk, and yellow mustard in a bowl. Add to the meat mixture and work it in thoroughly by hand until everything is evenly mixed.

4 Transfer the meat mixture to the loaf pan, rounding off the top very slightly and making a shallow furrow lengthwise down the center of the loaf. The meat should be at least ¾ inch below the top edge of the pan. If you have extra mixture, pack it into the ramekins.

5 FOR THE GLAZE: Combine the maple syrup, brown sugar, vinegar, mustard, and Worcestershire in a small saucepan. Heat, whisking, then remove from the heat as soon it begins to boil. Spoon one-third of the glaze over the loaf.

6 Bake the loaf on the middle oven rack for 45 minutes. Slide the loaf out of the oven and spoon another one-third of the glaze over the meat. Bake for another 45 minutes, or until the center of the loaf registers 165°F on an instant-read or meat thermometer. Transfer the loaf to a cooling rack and let cool for at least 30 minutes before slicing and serving. Rewarm the remaining glaze and spoon it over the slices when serving.

Roast Breast of Chicken with Red Wine–Blueberry Glaze

THE SHAKERS APPLIED the virtues of simplicity, purity, and perfection to their work and to themselves. For their cooking, that meant fresh ingredients, simply prepared, as in this wonderful dish from James Haller and Jeffrey Paige's *Cooking in the Shaker Spirit*, which, alas, is no longer in print.

Ingredients

Red Wine–Blueberry Glaze

- 1 pint fresh blueberries
- 1 cup red wine
- 1 cup pure maple syrup
- ¼ cup Dijon mustard

Roast Chicken

- 4 bone-in chicken breasts (1 pound each)
- ¼ cup chopped fresh flat-leaf parsley
- Salt and freshly ground black pepper
- Paprika
- Garlic powder

1 FOR THE GLAZE: Bring the blueberries, wine, maple syrup, and mustard to a boil in a medium saucepan. Decrease the heat to low and simmer until reduced by one-third, about 1 hour 15 minutes.

2 FOR THE CHICKEN: Preheat the oven to 400°F/200°C. Blot the chicken breasts dry with paper towels. Split the chicken breasts in half.

3 Place the chicken in a roasting pan and sprinkle with the parsley and as much salt, pepper, paprika, and garlic powder as you like. Roast the chicken for 30 minutes.

4 Remove the chicken from the oven and spread with the glaze. Return to the oven and cook for 10 minutes longer, or until the meat is tender and the juices run clear when the meat is pierced with a fork.

Main Dishes

Salmon with Mango Salsa

YIELD: 4 servings

SALMON CERTAINLY DOESN'T NEED much adornment, but a sauce or a salsa just seems to bring out the flavor of the fish. When I'm planning what to dress it up with, I'm torn between a simple Maple Glaze (page 111), Pineapple Salsa (page 89), or Mango Salsa. Sometimes I just let the greengrocer decide: If there isn't a beautiful, ripe pineapple or mango, it's the glaze. If both are available, well, sometimes I make two kinds of salsa and eat the fish with a little bit of each.

Ingredients

Mango Salsa

- 1 ripe mango, peeled, pitted, and chopped
- 1 small jalapeño, seeded and finely chopped
- 2 scallions, green part only, finely chopped
- Juice of 1 small lime (about 1 tablespoon)
- 1 tablespoon pure maple syrup

Salmon and Glaze

- 4 salmon fillets or steaks (about 6 ounces each)
- 2 tablespoons olive oil
- 2 tablespoons maple syrup
- 1½ tablespoons Dijon mustard
- 1½ tablespoons fresh lime juice
- 1 tablespoon (peeled) minced fresh gingerroot
- 2 cloves garlic, minced

---

1 FOR THE SALSA: Combine the mango, jalapeño, scallions, lime juice, and maple syrup in a small bowl. Refrigerate, covered, to allow the flavors to blend. (The salsa will keep for up to 2 days, refrigerated.)

2 FOR THE SALMON: Preheat the grill to medium-high (or preheat the broiler).

3 FOR THE GLAZE: Whisk together the oil, maple syrup, mustard, lime juice, gingerroot, and garlic. Set aside.

4 For salmon fillets, brush or spoon the glaze heavily over the flesh and set aside for 5 to 10 minutes. (If you're using steaks, coat both sides and set aside.) Grill the salmon skin side down for 4 to 5 minutes, then carefully turn and grill another 4 to 5 minutes, until done. Thicker salmon steaks will require 2 to 3 minutes longer than fillets. To oven broil, line a rimmed baking sheet with foil and coat with a little oil or nonstick cooking spray. Place the salmon on the foil — skin side down for fillets — and broil 4 to 5 inches from the heat. Fillets should take about 7 to 8 minutes, steaks a couple of minutes longer.

5 Transfer the salmon to a platter or dinner plates, spoon the salsa over it, and serve.

Chicken with Maple-Mustard Glaze

THIS RECIPE IS AN ADAPTATION of one developed by my late friend Richard Sax, who was a gifted cook, food writer, and all-around fine person. What he would do is make the sauce, minus the mustard, and brush it on the chicken. Then he would broil the chicken 6 inches from the heat, 15 minutes on each side, and brush the mustard on at the last minute. Here's my way, for the grill, but you could also broil it Richard's way.

Ingredients

- 1 broiler-fryer chicken (2½–3 pounds), cut up
- ¼ cup pure maple syrup
- 3 tablespoons Dijon mustard
- Juice of ½ small lemon (about 1 tablespoon)
- 2 teaspoons tamari or soy sauce
- 1 clove garlic, minced
- ½ teaspoon freshly ground black pepper

1 Trim the excess fat from the chicken, and blot dry with paper towels. Place the chicken in a large shallow casserole dish and set aside.

2 Combine the maple syrup, mustard, lemon juice, tamari, garlic, and pepper in a small saucepan; bring to a boil. Boil for 1 minute. Remove from the heat.

3 Brush the chicken on both sides with half the maple sauce. Refrigerate for 30 to 60 minutes.

4 Preheat the grill to medium-high. Grill, periodically turning and basting the chicken pieces with the remaining sauce, until the meat is tender and the juices run clear when the meat is pierced with a fork, about 15 minutes per side. Total cooking time will vary depending on the size of the pieces.

It is said that children have grown up in this country without tasting any but maple sugar.

— Susan Fenimore Cooper, *Rural Hours*, 1850

Sweet-and-Sour Chicken-Cashew Salad

THIS IS NOT SO MUCH the sort of chicken salad you'd put in a sandwich as it is something you'd arrange in the middle of a colorful plate of greens and serve for a light lunch or dinner. There are all sorts of contrasting flavors and textures here, much to the salad's advantage.

Ingredients

- ½ cup Spicy Sweet-and-Sour Dressing (page 82)
- 2 tablespoons tahini
- 2 cups bite-size chunks cooked chicken
- 1 stalk celery, finely chopped
- 2 scallions, thinly sliced
- ½ cup coarsely chopped cashews
- 1 tablespoon minced jalapeño, optional
- 1 lemon, halved
- Salt and freshly ground black pepper
- Greens for serving
- Minced raisins for garnish, optional

1 Put the salad dressing into a large bowl and thoroughly whisk in the tahini so the mixture thickens a little. Fold in the chicken, celery, scallions, cashews, and jalapeño, if desired.

2 Squeeze in a little lemon juice and sprinkle in some salt and pepper, then taste and adjust the seasonings to your liking. Cover and refrigerate until serving. Serve on a plate of greens, garnished very lightly with the raisins, if desired.

Flavor Options

Tahini, a sesame seed paste, is widely available in health food stores and many larger supermarkets. But you can vary the flavor of the chicken salad by skipping the tahini and substituting peanut butter or about a tablespoon of Dijon mustard.

Main Dishes

BEYOND BREAKFAST

107

Hot and Spicy Shrimp and Sausage Kabobs

YIELD: 4 servings

WHETHER OR NOT you agree with my friend Cindy — who called this the best meal of her entire life (she had a sheltered childhood) — I do think you'll be pleased. The heat can be regulated here by gauging the amount and type of chile peppers you use; for most folks, I find the 2 tablespoons of jalapeños sufficient. Of course, if you have a stash of fresh hot peppers that you fancy, use them instead. Good beer-drinking grub, this is. But if you're limiting your meat consumption, skewer up 2 pounds of shrimp and skip the sausage.

Ingredients

- 1¼ cups North Country Basting Sauce (page 83)
-    Juice of ½ medium lemon (about 1½ tablespoons)
- 2 tablespoons minced onion
- 2 tablespoons minced jalapeño
- 1 pound spicy, fully cooked sausage
- 1 pound large shrimp in the shell

1 Blend the basting sauce, lemon juice, onion, and jalapeño in a large bowl.

2 Cut the sausage into ½-inch slices and add to the marinade along with the shrimp. Stir to coat well. Cover and set aside for 1 hour; it may be refrigerated for several hours.

3 Preheat the grill to medium-high (or preheat the broiler). Thread four or five long skewers alternately with the shrimp and sausage. Either grill or broil, far enough from the heat to prevent charring, for about 10 minutes total or until the shrimp are pink. Turn occasionally during cooking and brush with more sauce. And be sure to tell your guests that the shrimp are in the shell.

The Lemonade Diet

Also known as the Master Cleanse fast or the lemon juice cure, this natural health regimen developed by Stanley Burroughs has maple syrup in the special lemonade recipe.

The drink is said to replenish vitamins and minerals during a fast, and maple syrup is rich in minerals. I make no claims for or against this practice, and you should consult your physician before trying it, but it sure is an interesting bit of maple trivia.

Four-Bean Bake with Hamburger

YIELD: 4 servings

VISITORS TO the Sugarbush Maple Syrup Festival at the Kortright Centre for Conservation in Woodbridge, Ontario, get a bonus with the guide they use to take a self-guided tour of the bush: maple recipes, including this one for a casserole that would travel well to a sugaring-off party or another potluck event.

Ingredients

½ pound lean ground beef
½ cup chopped onion
2 cups baked beans (one 16-ounce can)
1 cup canned cannellini beans, rinsed and drained
1 cup canned pinto beans, rinsed and drained
1 cup canned red kidney beans, rinsed and drained
6 tablespoons barbecue sauce
6 tablespoons pure maple syrup
3 teaspoons prepared mustard
Salt and freshly ground black pepper

1 Preheat the oven to 400°F/200°C. Sauté the ground beef and onion in a large heavy skillet for 4 to 5 minutes over medium-high heat.

2 Stir in the baked beans, cannellini beans, pinto beans, kidney beans, barbecue sauce, maple syrup, and mustard. Add salt and pepper to taste. Bring the mixture to a boil.

3 Transfer the mixture to a Dutch oven or casserole dish and bake for 20 to 30 minutes, stirring occasionally, until bubbly.

Mr. Jefferson, the Secretary of State[,] . . . thinks in a few years we shall be able to supply half the World [with maple syrup].

— Arthur Noble to Judge William Cooper, May 7, 1791

Maple Beef Teriyaki

YIELD: 8 main-course or 16 appetizer servings

ILONA SHERRATT, the illustration coordinator at Storey Publishing, was creating art for an earlier revision of this book around the same time she was asked to prepare food for a party. Her natural love of real maple syrup inspired her to use it as the base for this beef teriyaki. It was such a huge hit that my editor requested I include the recipe in the new edition. And so here it is.

Ingredients
- ¼ cup pure maple syrup
- ¼ cup tamari or soy sauce
- 2 tablespoons vegetable oil
- 2 tablespoons toasted sesame oil
- 1 tablespoon five-spice powder
- 2 pounds lean beef, sliced across the grain into ¼-inch strips

1 Mix the maple syrup, tamari, vegetable oil, sesame oil, and five-spice powder in a large nonreactive bowl. Add the beef and toss well to coat the meat.

2 Cover and refrigerate overnight; stir occasionally.

3 Preheat the grill to medium-high or preheat the broiler.

4 Drain the beef, discarding the excess marinade, and pat dry with paper towels. Thread the meat onto eight long or sixteen short skewers (if using wooden skewers, soak them in water for 30 minutes before threading on the beef).

5 Grill or broil the beef until tender, turning occasionally, about 6 minutes total for medium-rare.

Maple Glaze

When I eat breakfast out, it never ceases to amaze me how many people dip bacon, ham, or sausage into the maple syrup on the plate from their pancakes, waffles, or French toast.

Maple does have a way of bringing out the best in meats. To enhance the experience, add a few ingredients to maple syrup and you'll have a delicious glaze for a variety of meats, from ham, whole or in steaks, to pork tenderloin and chicken or turkey.

Just combine ¾ cup pure maple syrup, ¼ cup apple cider vinegar, 1 teaspoon dry mustard, and a pinch of ground cloves in a small saucepan. Bring the mixture to a boil. If you want to glaze meat while it's still roasting in the oven, boil the mixture for a minute or two, because it will thicken further in the oven. If you want to serve the glaze as a sauce, boil it for 3 to 5 minutes so it will thicken.

Be creative with your glaze: Use plum jam or soy sauce instead of the vinegar, or Dijon mustard instead of the dry mustard.

Crispy Maple Spareribs

ALL YOU NEED to make a meal of these is a big green salad — and plenty of napkins.

Ingredients

    3   pounds lean pork spareribs
    1   small onion, finely chopped
   ¾   cup pure maple syrup
    1   tablespoon chili sauce
    1   tablespoon red wine vinegar
    1   tablespoon Worcestershire sauce
   ¼   teaspoon dry mustard
        Salt and freshly ground black pepper

1 Preheat the oven to 400°F/200°C. Arrange the ribs on a wire rack in a roasting pan and roast for 30 minutes.

2 Combine the onion, maple syrup, chili sauce, vinegar, Worcestershire, mustard, and salt and pepper to taste in a small saucepan and bring to a boil; boil for 5 minutes.

3 Lower the oven temperature to 350°F/180°C. Remove the ribs from the rack and arrange in a baking pan; brush them with the sauce. Bake uncovered for 45 to 60 minutes, basting frequently, until the ribs are glazed to a deep mahogany color.

4 Cut between the rib bones with a sharp knife and serve.

Pork Magic

Pork and maple is my favorite combination, or at least I think so until I think about seafood and maple, poultry and maple, or, well, anything and maple. It's especially easy to indulge in pork and maple with the wider availability of so-tender-you-can-cut-it-with-a-fork pork tenderloin.

For a quick meal, cut the tenderloin crosswise into 1-inch slices, pound them into ¼-inch medallions, and sprinkle them with dried sage or rosemary. Dredge lightly in flour if desired, and sauté in a little butter and olive oil. Serve with warm maple syrup or with a dipping sauce of maple syrup and melted crabapple jelly.

It takes little imagination to vary the dish: Add chopped fresh gingerroot when you cook the meat; sprinkle dried cranberries or toasted nuts over the medallions before serving; or top with fruit salsa.

Maple Vinegar–Roasted Pork

JOHN BOYAJIAN tells a great and colorful tale about the serendipitous path that took him from graduate-school studies in education to the food business — from importing caviar and smoked salmon to producing top-quality flavored oils and vinegars. His recipe for pork tenderloin gets maple flavor from his maple vinegar, and its lovely touch of herb from his oil infused with rosemary.

Ingredients

- ½ cup rosemary oil
- ¼ cup maple vinegar (Mail-Order Sources, page 172)
- 3 cloves garlic, finely chopped
- 1 tablespoon Dijon mustard
- 1 tablespoon pure maple syrup
- 2 pork tenderloins (¾ pound each)
  Salt and freshly ground black pepper
  Cranberry or other chutney, optional

---

1 Combine the oil, vinegar, garlic, mustard, and maple syrup in a large nonreactive bowl. Add the pork and turn to coat with the marinade. Cover and refrigerate for 8 hours or overnight, turning and basting the pork a few times.

2 Preheat the oven to 375°F/190°C. Drain the pork, discarding the excess marinade. Place the pork in a roasting pan and season with salt and pepper.

3 Roast for 20 to 30 minutes, until an instant-read or meat thermometer inserted into the center of the tenderloins registers 155°F/70°C. Remove from the oven and let stand for 15 minutes. (The tenderloins may also be grilled over medium heat for approximately 10 minutes per side.)

4 Slice thinly and serve with cranberry chutney, if desired.

Kortright Centre for Conservation

JUST ABOUT EVERY SUGARMAKER has had to boil sap through the night at least once. Visitors to the Kortright Centre for Conservation in Woodbridge, Ontario, get a feel for that ritual in a "Maple Syrup by Lamplight" hike through Kortright's sugar bush. The event also includes a campfire visit with a warm treat. The sugar bush is part of Kortright's 800 acres of green space, where the Toronto and Region Conservation Authority provides environmental learning opportunities.

But during Kortright's six-week Sugarbush Maple Syrup Festival, visitors can take self-guided tours of the sugar bush. Visitors see the history and the process of sugar making on the walk. One display shows the gash in the tree and the twig, inserted into the cut, that allows sap to run into a birch bark container, which Native Americans would have used to collect sap. Another exhibit is of a modern gravity-fed tube system. There's a pioneer sugar camp set up as one would have been in the nineteenth century and a modern sugar shack that houses an evaporator.

"People enjoy trying on the wooden yoke and two buckets that were used to carry sap from the trees to the sugarhouse, and getting samples of sap and syrup so they can taste the difference," said Wendy Heron, special events coordinator at Kortright.

They can also eat pancakes at the Visitor Centre, and, if they were enraptured by the magic of making maple syrup, they can buy a do-it-yourself syrup-making kit. (Kortright's recipe for Four-Bean Bake with Hamburger is on page 110.)

Ham Steak in Rum-Raisin Sauce

YIELD: 2–3 servings

HERE'S A SIMPLE, tasty way to prepare ham steaks. Try this with biscuits and Braised Onions with Bacon (page 88).

Ingredients

- 1 pound ham steak
- 1 cup apple cider
- ¼ cup plus 2 tablespoons pure maple syrup
- ¼ cup dark rum
- 2–3 tablespoons orange juice, preferably freshly squeezed
- ½ cup raisins

---

1 Preheat the oven to 350°F/180°C. Put the ham steak in a shallow casserole dish slightly larger than the steak.

2 Bring the cider, ¼ cup of the maple syrup, the rum, orange juice, and raisins to a near boil in a small saucepan. Cover and let sit for 10 minutes. Remove the raisins with a slotted spoon, put them in a small bowl, and spoon enough of the hot liquid over them to cover completely. Pour the remaining liquid over the ham and bake for 1 hour.

3 When the hour is up, remove the ham from the oven and preheat the broiler.

4 Combine the raisins and their soaking liquid in a food processor or blender with several tablespoons of the casserole juice and the remaining 2 tablespoons maple syrup. Process briefly — a little roughness is good — and pour it directly over the ham. Place the ham under the broiler for just a few moments, until it sizzles and browns; keep a close eye on it.

There's no finer sight or smell in Spring than steam billowing from a sugar shack.

— Charlie Tetreault, *Log Cabin Chronicles*

Gingered Pork Medallions

A QUICK SKILLET RECIPE, this dish with Asian flavors can be made with pork tenderloins, cut crosswise into ½-inch-thick pieces and then pounded as described below, or boneless chicken breasts. Serve it with rice and a salad of snow peas and radishes with an orange vinaigrette.

Ingredients

- 4 boneless pork chops, ¾ inch thick
- ⅓ cup unbleached all-purpose flour
- ½ teaspoon salt
- ¼ teaspoon freshly ground black pepper
- 2 tablespoons butter
- 2 shallots, thinly sliced
- 1 tablespoon peeled and finely chopped fresh gingerroot
- 1 clove garlic, finely chopped
- ½ cup dry white wine or chicken broth
- ¼ cup pure maple syrup
- ¼ cup teriyaki sauce
- 2 tablespoons rice vinegar

1 Using a meat mallet or rolling pin, flatten the pork chops between sheets of waxed paper or plastic wrap to a thickness of about ¼ inch.

2 Combine the flour, salt, and pepper in a shallow dish. Melt 1 tablespoon of the butter in a large heavy skillet over medium-high heat. Dredge the pork in the flour mixture, shaking off the excess. Add two of the pork chops to the skillet and sauté until brown and cooked through, about 2 minutes per side. Transfer to a platter and keep warm by covering loosely with aluminum foil. Repeat with the remaining 1 tablespoon butter and two pork chops.

3 Decrease the heat to medium. Add the shallots, gingerroot, and garlic to the pan and sauté for 2 minutes. Stir in the wine, maple syrup, teriyaki, and vinegar. Cook, uncovered, stirring occasionally, until the sauce thickens slightly, 5 to 7 minutes. Return the pork to the pan and heat through.

Main Dishes

four

Maple
Sweets

n this chapter, you'll find a heavenly assortment
of treats that explore and exploit the sweeten-
ing power and delectable flavor of maple. Pile
almond or chocolate bar cookies on a platter or
fill your cookie jar with spicy or gingery gems. Or
delight your family with the mouthwatering odors
of maple pies and cakes baking in the oven, the
creamy goodness of maple-inspired ice cream, or
a maple-infused coffee shake.

Gorp Bars

GOOD OLD RAISIN and peanut bars. Moist and chewy, they travel well and are great for brown baggers and hikers.

Ingredients

- 1 cup unsalted, unsweetened peanut butter (smooth or crunchy)
- ½ cup (1 stick) butter, softened
- 1 cup pure maple syrup
- 1 egg
- 1 teaspoon vanilla extract
- ½ teaspoon baking soda
- 1 cup old-fashioned rolled oats
- 1 cup whole-wheat or unbleached all-purpose flour
- 1½ cups finely chopped unsalted raw peanuts
- 1½ cups raisins or dried cranberries

1 Preheat the oven to 350°F/180°C. Grease a 9- by 13-inch baking pan.

2 Cream the peanut butter and butter with an electric mixer. Gradually add the maple syrup, egg, vanilla, and baking soda. Stir in the oats and flour, just to blend, followed by the peanuts and raisins. Using floured hands, pat the mixture evenly into the prepared pan.

3 Bake for about 30 minutes, just until the edges begin to brown. Let cool on a wire rack before cutting into bars.

Whoever would have thought that we would derive such pleasure from tree sap?

—Daniel Boileau

Black-Bottom Cheesecake Bars

YIELD: About 24 bars

I DON'T MIX CHOCOLATE with maple syrup too often, because chocolate tends to overpower the subtle taste of maple. When I do, though — such as in these scrumptious cheesecake bars — I really like to go all out. I find that since the chocolate ends up underneath, you can still appreciate the maple-flavored cheese layer. These are excellent.

Ingredients

- 1 recipe Rich Maple Short Crust (page 124)
- 1 pound cream cheese, softened
- ½ cup sour cream, at room temperature
- 2 eggs, at room temperature
- ¾ cup pure maple syrup, at room temperature
- 1 teaspoon vanilla extract
- 1 teaspoon lemon juice (from half of a small lemon)
- 1½–2 cups semisweet chocolate chips

---

1 Prepare the short crust as directed and spread in a 9- by 13-inch baking pan. Preheat the oven to 400°F/200°C.

2 Beat the cream cheese with an electric mixer until fairly light in texture. Beat in the sour cream and then the eggs, one at a time. Gradually beat in the maple syrup, followed by the vanilla and lemon juice.

3 Sprinkle the chocolate chips evenly over the crust. Slowly pour on the cheese mixture. Bake for 15 minutes, then lower the oven temperature to 350°F/180°C and bake for 30 minutes longer. The cake will be puffy and probably will have developed cracks on the top.

4 Let cool on a wire rack, cover, then chill before cutting into bars.

Bars, Cookies & Candy

MAPLE SWEETS

Dreamy Almond Bars

YIELD: 24–36 bars

THESE BARS ARE ENTIRELY out of the question if you value your waistline. You could easily put on several pounds just *reading* this recipe, let alone eating it. On the other hand, this makes a large batch, to be cut into small pieces, so you could stash away a piece or two for yourself and put out the rest for a Christmas or New Year's gathering. I specify a 10- by 15-inch jelly-roll pan, but I have also used an 11- by 17-inch pan. It's not a difficult recipe, but you should read the instructions through before starting, just to be sure of the technique.

Ingredients

Crust

- 1 cup (2 sticks) butter, softened
- ½ cup firmly packed brown sugar
- 1 egg, at room temperature
- 3 cups unbleached all-purpose flour

Topping

- ½ cup (1 stick) butter
- ¾ cup pure maple syrup
- ½ cup firmly packed brown sugar
- ¼ cup honey
- ¼ cup heavy cream
- 2 cups chopped almonds
- 1 teaspoon vanilla extract

1 FOR THE CRUST: Preheat the oven to 375°F/190°C. Lightly grease a 10- by 15-inch jelly-roll pan.

2 Cream the butter and sugar in a large bowl. When light, beat in the egg. Add the flour, about ½ cup at a time, working it in with a wooden spoon. Divide the dough into four pieces and put a piece in each quadrant of the jelly-roll pan.

3 Push the dough into the pan with floured hands, forming a seamless crust. Keep it as even as you can and work it up the sides to the top of the rim. It won't look perfect, but just do the best job you can; if you want to flatten it out some, roll it with a pin. Cover with plastic wrap and chill for 15 minutes. Poke the dough three or four times with a fork, then bake for 15 minutes. Let cool on a wire rack. Mix a tiny amount of flour and water together to make a thick paste, and rub a little into the fork holes to close them up.

4 FOR THE TOPPING: After the crust has cooled for about 20 minutes, melt the butter in a large saucepan. Add the maple syrup, sugar, and honey and bring to a boil. When it boils, add the cream and bring back to a boil. Boil for 2 minutes. Quickly remove from the heat and stir in the almonds and vanilla. Spread evenly over the crust. Bake for 20 minutes; it will bubble and darken somewhat. Let cool thoroughly on a wire rack, then cut into bars.

Rich Maple Short Crust

THIS IS A GOOD, maple-laced bar-cookie crust that's a cinch to prepare. I use it, among other things, for Black-Bottom Cheesecake Bars (page 121).

Ingredients
- ¾ cup (1½ sticks) butter, softened
- ⅓ cup pure maple syrup, at room temperature
- ½ teaspoon vanilla extract
- 2 cups unbleached all-purpose flour
- ½ teaspoon salt

1 Cream the butter with an electric mixer in a medium bowl. Continue to beat, gradually adding the maple syrup and vanilla. Combine the flour and salt, then gradually add to the creamed mixture, working it in with a wooden spoon.

2 Using floured hands, pat evenly into a 9- by 13-inch baking pan; roll with a can or bottle to even it out. Cover, then refrigerate until needed.

Beyond Syrup: Maple Products

Besides maple syrup and maple sugar, there are several other traditional products made and sold by sugarmakers.

Maple cream. Also called maple butter, this is produced by heating maple syrup, cooling it, then stirring until a creamy, thick consistency is reached. It's excellent on toast, bagels, doughnuts, and more, and may be used as a cake frosting.

Maple candy. For candies, the syrup is cooked about 10°F/6°C hotter than for maple cream, then poured into molds.

Maple sugar. This granulated variety is made by continuing to boil down syrup past the candy stage, until crystallization takes place.

Maple vinegar. Wonderful for marinades and deglazing pans, maple vinegar was traditionally made with sap from the very end of the sugaring season. Syrup made from that sap contains metabolites, nutrients that will feed the leaf buds, and has off flavors that are not desirable for retail sales.

Maple-Spice Cookies

SIMPLE BUT SPECIAL, these cookies were created by Sue Clark of Wells, Vermont, who has won many maple cooking and baking contests. George Cook, maple specialist at the University of Vermont Extension, says Sue and her husband, Bill, are "truly a maple couple." Bill's sugar-making story is on page 136.

Ingredients

- 1 cup vegetable shortening
- 1 cup firmly packed brown sugar
- ½ cup granulated sugar, plus more for topping
- ½ cup Grade A Dark Robust maple syrup
- 2 eggs
- 4 cups unbleached all-purpose flour
- 2¼ teaspoons baking soda
- 2 teaspoons ground ginger
- 1½ teaspoons ground cinnamon
- ¼ teaspoon salt

1 Preheat the oven to 350°F/180°C. Grease a baking sheet. Cream the shortening, brown sugar, and granulated sugar in a large bowl with an electric mixer until fluffy. Beat in the maple syrup and the eggs, one egg at a time.

2 In a separate medium bowl, combine the flour, baking soda, ginger, cinnamon, and salt. Add the flour mixture to the shortening mixture, a little at a time, and mix until well blended. The dough will be sticky.

3 Sprinkle granulated sugar onto a sheet of waxed paper. Roll the dough into 1½-inch balls and dip the tops into the sugar. Place the balls 2 inches apart on the baking sheet.

4 Bake for 12 to 13 minutes, until light golden brown and the center is set; do not overbake. Let cool on the baking sheet for 1 minute. Transfer to a wire rack to cool completely. Repeat with the remaining dough.

Coffee Chip Cookies

THIS IS A CLASSIC chocolate chip cookie recipe from my original self-published maple book. It incorporates almost all of my gustatory weaknesses — butter, maple, coffee, chocolate, and walnuts — and, I suspect, accounts for no small share of my dentist's annual income. Dedicated to my friend Cindy, who'll take her coffee any way she can.

Ingredients

- 1 cup (2 sticks) butter, softened
- 1 cup pure maple syrup, at room temperature
- 1½ tablespoons instant espresso powder or instant coffee
- 2 tablespoons hot water
- 2 teaspoons vanilla extract or almond extract
- 1½ cups whole-wheat flour
- 1 cup unbleached all-purpose flour
- 2 cups finely chopped walnuts
- 1 teaspoon baking soda
- ½ teaspoon salt
- 1½ cups semisweet chocolate chips

1 Preheat the oven to 350°F/180°C. Grease a baking sheet. Cream the butter in a large bowl with an electric mixer, slowly drizzling in the maple syrup. Dissolve the espresso powder in the hot water and beat that in, along with the vanilla.

2 In a separate bowl, toss the flours, walnuts, baking soda, and salt to mix. Stir into the creamed mixture, in several stages, until the flour is incorporated. Stir in the chocolate chips; don't beat the batter.

3 Let the batter sit for several minutes, then drop slightly mounded tablespoons of batter onto the baking sheet, leaving about 2 inches between the mounds. Bake for about 15 minutes — only one sheet at a time — just until the edges begin to brown. Transfer to a wire rack to cool. Repeat with the remaining batter.

Maple-Pumpkin Cookies

YIELD: About 36 cookies

HERE'S A SOFT, rather unusual cookie, packed with autumn highlights and a whisper of spice. The cookies have a light, cakey texture, so you can easily put away five or six at a sitting. Great with cider or a cold glass of milk.

Ingredients

- 1 cup pure maple syrup
- 1 cup pumpkin purée, canned or freshly cooked and cooled
- 1 egg
- 1 teaspoon vanilla extract
- ½ cup (1 stick) butter, softened
- 1 cup unbleached all-purpose flour
- 1 cup whole-wheat flour
- 1 teaspoon baking powder
- 1 teaspoon baking soda
- ½ teaspoon ground cinnamon
- ½ teaspoon ground nutmeg
- ½ teaspoon salt
- ½ cup chopped pecans
- 1 cup peeled and grated apple

1 Preheat the oven to 350°F/180°C. Grease a baking sheet. Combine the maple syrup, pumpkin purée, egg, and vanilla in a food processor and process until smooth. Cream the butter with an electric mixer, then stir in about half of the pumpkin mixture.

2 In a separate bowl, toss together the flours, baking powder, baking soda, cinnamon, nutmeg, and salt.

3 Add the flour mixture and the remaining pumpkin mixture alternately to the butter mixture, stirring after each addition just until blended. Fold in the pecans and apple.

4 Spoon heaping tablespoons of the batter, 2 inches apart, onto the prepared baking sheet. Bake for 15 to 20 minutes, until the bottom edges just start to brown. Transfer to a wire rack to cool. Repeat with the remaining batter.

Blonde Ginger Cutout Cookies

THESE ARE A LOT like gingerbread cookies. They're my kids' favorite cookie to make, and they cut them into all sorts of shapes. It's important to chill the dough for at least two hours before you roll it, otherwise it will be difficult to handle.

Ingredients

- ⅔ cup vegetable shortening
- ⅓ cup (5⅓ tablespoons) butter, softened
- 1 cup pure maple syrup, at room temperature
- 1 tablespoon blackstrap molasses
- ½ teaspoon vanilla extract
- 4 cups unbleached all-purpose or whole-wheat flour
- 2 teaspoons baking soda
- ½ teaspoon salt
- ½ teaspoon ground ginger
- ¼ teaspoon ground cloves
- ¼ teaspoon ground nutmeg

1 Cream together the shortening and butter in a large bowl with an electric mixer. Gradually beat in the maple syrup, molasses, and vanilla.

2 In a separate large bowl, mix the flour, baking soda, salt, ginger, cloves, and nutmeg. Work this into the creamed mixture, about 1 cup at a time. Using floured hands, divide the dough in half and wrap each half in plastic wrap, each flattened into a disk. Chill for at least 2 hours.

3 Preheat the oven to 350°F/180°C. Lightly grease a baking sheet. Roll the dough out, one part at a time, onto a sheet of waxed paper; make it a little less than ¼ inch thick. Cut into whatever shapes you like, transfer to the baking sheet, and bake for 10 to 12 minutes, until the bottoms are golden. Let cool briefly on the baking sheet, then transfer to a wire rack to cool completely. Repeat with the remaining dough.

The Real Thing: Butter

When it comes to cooking, maple syrup is not the only real thing that matters. I use real butter — unsalted — because it gives me more control over the final flavor of a dish. If you use salted butter, reduce the salt called for in the dish or in whatever you're baking (there's about ⅜ teaspoon of salt in a stick of butter).

Maple Syrup Candies

IF YOU CRAVE the sweet maple candies sold at tourist shops, you need not wait until your next vacation to enjoy them. Maple syrup producers' associations are eager to share these treats, and how to make them at home, to spread the gospel of pure maple syrup. This recipe is from the Vermont Maple Sugar Makers Association/Vermont Maple Promotion Board; the Massachusetts Maple Producers Association has produced a helpful video about making maple cream and maple candy. If you haven't tried these maple candies, be forewarned: They're like no other treat you've ever experienced.

Ingredients

2 cups pure light-grade maple syrup (Grade A Golden Delicate)

A few drops of vegetable oil or butter

1 Fill a large pot partially with water. Bring to a boil, and note the temperature of the boiling water with a candy thermometer. (Since water boils at different temperatures in different locations, it is important to follow this step.) Set some candy molds into a jelly-roll pan. Set aside. (If using metal or wood molds, lightly grease them.)

2 Empty the large pot and place the syrup in it. Add a few drops of oil. (Boiling maple syrup will foam up; the oil keeps the foam down. Buttering the rim of the pot will also help.)

3 Boil carefully over high heat, without stirring, until the temperature of the boiling syrup is 28°F/17°C above the boiling point of your water (212°F/100°C at sea level).

4 Remove from the heat and let cool for 3 to 5 minutes. Do not stir or disturb the candy at this point; if the thermometer is attached to the pan, leave it there during the cooling period.

5 Stir evenly until the liquid loses its gloss, starts to become opaque, and begins to thicken. (This is the tricky part; if you stir too long the thickened syrup will "set up," or harden, in the pan. If this happens, add a cup of water, and reheat slowly to dissolve the sugar, then start over. But if you don't stir long enough, the sugar may not "set up" in the molds at all.)

6 Carefully pour the candy into the molds. It's helpful to have an assistant spread the syrup in the molds while you continue to pour the mixture into the other molds.

7 Allow the candies to cool, remove from the molds, place on a rack to dry for a few hours, and enjoy.

Candy Molds

There are many choices for candy molds. Rubber molds work best for maple syrup candy, but lightly greased metal and wood molds also work well. Even small disposable aluminum foil pans, lightly greased, can be used. Candy molds may be purchased at many craft stores, some department stores, and from specialty kitchen shops, catalogs, or websites.

Candied Popcorn and Nuts

YIELD: About 2½ quarts

MY GENERATION GREW UP ON a mass-market version of this, and frankly I don't remember if it was the sweet popcorn or the prize at the bottom of the box we liked more. This maple version makes a special Christmas gift when packed into festive bags. Try to enlist the help of a second person to support the pot while you scrape the boiled liquid into the popcorn mix.

Ingredients
- 2 cups walnuts or other nuts
- 1 cup raw (untoasted) sunflower seeds
- 2 quarts popped popcorn, unsalted and unbuttered
- 1½ cups sugar
- ¾ cup pure maple syrup
- ½ cup water
- 4 tablespoons butter
- ½ teaspoon salt
- 1 teaspoon ground cinnamon
- 1 teaspoon vanilla extract

1 You will need three baking sheets for this; grease two of them very lightly and set aside. Preheat the oven to 350°F/180°C.

2 Spread the nuts and seeds on the third baking sheet. In the preheated oven, toast the nuts and seeds for 7 minutes, stirring once. Turn off the oven. Remove the baking sheet; spread the popcorn on top of the nuts and seeds. Return to the oven to keep warm.

3 Bring the sugar, maple syrup, water, butter, and salt to a boil in a medium pot. Boil, partially covered, until the mixture reaches 290°F/145°C on a candy thermometer. Remove from the heat and stir in the cinnamon and vanilla.

4 Quickly transfer the popcorn mix to the largest bowl you have and pour in the hot liquid. Working quickly — it will soon stiffen — stir to coat the entire mixture. Spread on the greased baking sheets and let cool for 30 minutes. Break the mixture apart; store in plastic bags or tins.

Maple Fudge

A SPECIALTY OF SUGARHOUSES
and tourist shops all over maple
country, maple fudge is delicious but
requires a good sense of timing. If you
don't work quickly enough, you could
be eating it out of the pot.

Ingredients

- 2 cups sugar
- 1 cup pure maple syrup, preferably Grade A Golden
  Delicate
- ½ cup light cream
- 2 tablespoons butter

1 Grease an 8-inch square pan generously. Combine the
sugar, maple syrup, cream, and butter in a medium saucepan. Cook, stirring, over medium-high heat, until boiling.

2 Clip a candy thermometer to the side of the pan and
continue cooking and stirring until the mixture reaches
238°F/115°C, 10 to 15 minutes. Remove from the heat and let
cool, without stirring, until lukewarm (110°F/45°C), about
1 hour.

3 Remove the candy thermometer and beat the mixture
with a wooden spoon until the color lightens, the mixture
loses its gloss, and the fudge begins to set. Quickly press
into the prepared pan; score into squares while warm.
When the fudge is firm, cut into squares. Store tightly
covered.

Sugar on Snow

THERE IS NOTHING MORE authentically traditional among sugarmakers than a springtime sugar-on-snow party. It is actually an easy-to-make treat year-round, according to the Vermont Maple Sugar Makers Association, which distributes these guidelines. Sugar on snow is traditionally served with sour pickles and plain doughnuts to cut the sweetness of the candy.

Ingredients
- 1 quart pure maple syrup
- 1 cup (2 sticks) butter
- 1 tub packed snow or well-crushed ice (size depends on number being served; can be as small as a quart, but increase accordingly)

1 Heat the syrup and butter in a large pot over medium heat, watching carefully; turn the heat down if it threatens to boil over.

2 When a candy thermometer reaches 234°F/110°C, let cool slightly and test by spooning a tablespoon of syrup over the snow. If the syrup sits on top of the snow and clings to a fork like taffy, it's ready.

3 Pack the snow into bowls and pour the maple mixture in ribbons over the top.

Grandma stood by the brass kettle and with the big wooden spoon she poured hot syrup on each plate of snow. It cooled into soft candy, and as fast as it cooled, they ate it. They could eat all they wanted, for maple sugar never hurt anybody.

— Laura Ingalls Wilder, *Little House in the Big Woods*

Bill Clark

BILL CLARK is responsible, not once but twice, for a renewed interest in maple syrup. Back in the 1800s, just about every farm in Vermont had a maple orchard, and the Clark farm in Wells was no exception. But Bill's great-grandfather sold the maple lumber in 1893 to buy spruce lumber for a new barn. By the time Bill was 12 and his brother 10 years old, "there was a good maple orchard again." Fortuitously, school was shut down for a few weeks for what was called a "mud vacation." Bill and his brother went to the woods with 85 taps and made 15 gallons of syrup. Thus began the first maple renaissance.

In 1961, at a time when Bill says "the maple industry was going downhill in Vermont," he was "surprisingly" elected president of the Rutland County Maple Producers Association. Eight years later, he was elected president of the Vermont Maple Sugar Makers Association, a position he held for 32 years. "And sugaring is alive and well and a thriving industry today," Bill exclaims.

Bill and his wife, Sue, whose four kids "put in their hours and their days," have scaled back production on their farm. "After hosting 40,000 visitors from 6 continents over the years, I've reached the age where I don't need all that entertainment," Bill said, recalling the tourists who crowded the farm to watch him in the sugarhouse and who bought maple products and Sue's jams and jellies, as well as the years traveling the farmers' market circuit and serving the maple industry.

Bill's service has been well recognized. He's a member of the Maple Hall of Fame at the American Maple Museum in Croghan, New York, and the Vermont legislature honored him as "Vermont's very special Mr. Maple" when he retired from the association.

Maple-Apple Pie

YIELD: 8–10 servings

THIS IS YOUR BASIC maple-apple pie with a small twist of lime, just enough to complement the maple flavor. It's a very full pie and it needs to bake for a long time; don't be tempted to pull it out of the oven until the juices bubble thickly. You may substitute lemon for the lime if you'd like.

Ingredients

- ½ recipe Flaky Butter Crust (page 144) or other pie dough
- 8 cups peeled, cored, and thinly sliced cooking apples (about 6 large)
- ½ cup pure maple syrup
- 1½ tablespoons cornstarch
- ½ teaspoon finely grated lime zest
  Juice of ½ lime (about 1 tablespoon)
- 2 tablespoons butter, cut into bits
- 1 recipe Oat-Crumb Topping (page 165)

1 Prepare the pastry and line a 9-inch pie plate with it. Form a decorative raised edge and freeze. Preheat the oven to 425°F/220°C.

2 Put the sliced apples in a large bowl and pour on the maple syrup. Stir to coat the slices. Sift the cornstarch over the apples, stirring as you do so. Mix in the lime zest and juice. Turn the apples into the chilled crust and pat with your hands into an even mound. Dot with the butter. Cover the pie with loosely tented aluminum foil. Place the pie on a baking sheet and bake, on the center rack, for 20 minutes. Lower the oven temperature to 375°F/190°C and bake for 10 minutes longer.

3 Remove the foil cover and evenly distribute the topping over the top. Bake for another 45 to 60 minutes, until the juices bubble out thickly. If the top starts to get too dark, cover loosely with the foil. Let cool on a rack.

Maple-Pecan Pie

SWEET, RICH, and unabashedly decadent, this should be the standard against which all pecan pies are measured. Serve with vanilla ice cream.

Ingredients

- ½ recipe Flaky Butter Crust (page 144) or other pie dough
- 3 eggs, at room temperature
- 1 cup pure maple syrup, at room temperature
- ½ cup firmly packed brown sugar
- Pinch of salt
- 1 teaspoon vanilla extract
- 1 tablespoon unbleached all-purpose flour
- 1⅔ cups pecan halves

---

1 Prepare the pie shell according to the directions, line a 9-inch pie plate with the pastry, and refrigerate. Preheat the oven to 425°F/220°C.

2 Beat the eggs on high speed with an electric mixer for 2 minutes. Add the maple syrup, sugar, salt, vanilla, and flour and beat for another minute. Spread the pecans in the pie shell, then slowly pour in the egg mixture.

3 Bake on the center rack of the oven for 10 minutes. Lower the oven temperature to 375°F/190°C, and bake for about another 30 minutes. When done, the pie will be golden, puffed, and not soupy in the middle. Let cool on a rack before slicing.

Shaker Boiled Cider Pie

BOILED CIDER is little known today, but this pie is so good that it may spark a revival. The pie filling is like a rich maple-apple custard with a very thin layer of meringue on top. Possibly my favorite pie to date, it's great with vanilla ice cream or whipped cream.

Boiled Cider

The Shakers once used boiled cider as a primary sweetener because it was more economical for them than refined sugar. You can make your own boiled cider by reducing 7 cups of fresh, preservative-free cider to 1 cup, boiling it in a large enameled or stainless steel pot. But I generally just buy mine by the quart from Willis and Tina Wood at Wood's Cider Mill (Mail-Order Sources, page 172). Their family has been making it for more than a hundred years; they are one of the few remaining producers in the United States.

Ingredients

- ½ recipe Flaky Butter Crust (page 144) or other pie dough
- ¾ cup boiled cider
- ¾ cup pure maple syrup
- 2 tablespoons butter
- Pinch of salt
- 3 eggs, separated and at room temperature
- ⅛ teaspoon ground nutmeg

1 Prepare the pie shell according to the directions and line a 9-inch pie plate with the pastry. Form a slightly raised edge and place in the freezer. Preheat the oven to 350°F/180°C.

2 Gently warm the boiled cider, maple syrup, and butter in a small saucepan, just until the butter melts. Transfer to a large bowl and let cool slightly. Whisk in the salt and egg yolks.

3 Beat the egg whites in a clean dry bowl until stiff peaks form, then quickly whisk them into the cider mixture.

4 Pour the filling into the chilled crust and bake on the center rack of the oven for about 40 minutes. When done, the top will be dark brown and the pie will wobble just slightly, not in waves. Let cool on a rack, then dust the surface with the nutmeg. Serve slightly warm, or refrigerate and serve cold, which is the way I like it best.

Note: If you cover this pie, form an aluminum foil tent that doesn't touch the pie, or it will stick to the delicate meringue.

French Canadian Maple Sugar Pie

YIELD: 8–10 servings

RICHARD SAX, my late friend, credited this recipe to a Quebec cousin-of-a-friend. He described this, quite aptly, as something like pecan pie with a nice tart edge. It's really excellent with vanilla ice cream. Where the recipe calls for brewed tea, I like to use lemon herbal tea.

Ingredients

- ½ recipe Flaky Butter Crust (page 144) or other pie dough
- 3 eggs
- ¾ cup plus 2 tablespoons firmly packed brown sugar
- ¾ cup pure maple syrup
- 6 tablespoons butter, melted
- ¼ cup brewed tea
- 2 tablespoons plus ½ teaspoon apple cider vinegar
- Pinch of salt
- ¾ cup coarsely chopped walnuts

1 Prepare the pie shell according to the directions, line a 9-inch pie plate with the pastry, and refrigerate or freeze. Preheat the oven to 450°F/230°C.

2 Whisk together the eggs and sugar in a large bowl. Add the maple syrup, butter, tea, vinegar, and salt, whisking until smooth. Stir in the walnuts. Place the pie shell on a heavy baking sheet and pour in the filling.

3 Bake on the center rack of the oven for 10 minutes. Lower the oven temperature to 350°F/180°C and continue to bake for about 25 minutes longer, or until the center is set. Let cool on a wire rack. This pie is good warm, at room temperature, or cold.

Using Maple Sugar

Maple sugar, the sweetening staple of Native American and colonial diets, is sold in brick form and as granules, and it may be purchased by mail or Internet order from maple producers.

It can be substituted in most recipes that call for granulated white or brown sugar. But the maple sugar granules are larger than those of refined sugar, which sometimes causes cakes to crack. If you want to use maple sugar in a cake, grind the sugar into smaller granules in a food processor.

Pies & Cakes

MAPLE SWEETS

Sweet Potato Pie

THIS IS EASY, and there's very little cleanup because the whole thing is mixed right in a food processor. Instead of the sweet potato purée, you could use an equal amount of winter squash purée, or even canned cold-pack pure pumpkin.

Ingredients

½ recipe Flaky Butter Crust (page 144), partially baked and cooled (step 9, page 145)

2 cups sweet potato purée (bake potatoes, then purée flesh)

3 eggs, at room temperature

1 cup light cream

½ cup pure maple syrup, at room temperature

1 tablespoon blackstrap molasses

1 teaspoon ground cinnamon

1 teaspoon ground allspice

1 teaspoon ground ginger

¼ teaspoon salt

---

1 Prepare the pie shell, line a 9-inch pie plate with the pastry, and prebake according to the directions. Cool and refrigerate. Preheat the oven to 425°F/220°C.

2 Combine the sweet potato purée, eggs, cream, maple syrup, molasses, cinnamon, allspice, ginger, and salt in a food processor or blender and purée until smooth. Place the pie shell on a baking sheet and pour in the filling.

3 Bake on the center rack of the oven for 15 minutes. Lower the oven temperature to 350°F/180°C and bake for another 30 minutes, or until a sharp knife inserted in the center of the pie comes out clean. Don't worry if the surface of the pie develops a crack; that's fine. Let cool on a wire rack. Serve warm, at room temperature, or chilled.

Powdered Maple

Just as technology has improved the efficiency of sugaring, so it also has produced a method to dehydrate maple syrup into a powder. Reconstituting it takes only minutes; the powder is available by mail order.

Flaky Butter Crust

YIELD: Enough for 1 double-crust 9-inch pie
or 2 single-crust 9-inch pies

EVERYBODY HAS HIS OR HER
own special recipe for piecrust; this
is one of mine. Made with both butter
and a little vegetable shortening, it
is flavorful and flaky. The little bit
of lemon juice tenderizes the crust,
so it's noticeably delicate. If you are
using this for a top and bottom crust,
make one half slightly larger than the
other. Because so many of the pies in
this book go from freezer to oven, it
is important to use a metal or Pyrex
pie plate.

Ingredients
- 2½ cups unbleached all-purpose flour
- ½ teaspoon salt
- ¾ cup (1½ sticks) cold butter, cut into ¼-inch pieces
- ¼ cup vegetable shortening
- 1 tablespoon sugar
- 1 egg, cold
- 2 tablespoons ice water
- 1 tablespoon lemon juice or white vinegar

1 Combine the flour and salt in a large bowl and toss to
mix. Cut the butter and vegetable shortening into the flour
until the butter is evenly distributed, with pieces of fat no
larger than split peas. Add the sugar and toss with your fingers to incorporate.

2 Beat the egg, water, and lemon juice with a fork in a separate bowl. Drizzle half of this liquid over the flour, tossing
the mixture with a fork. Add the rest of the liquid, tossing
and blending as you pour. Work the mixture briefly with
your fork, then try to pack the dough together, like a snowball. If dry spots remain, use wet fingertips to pull them
into the ball of dough.

3 Divide the dough in half and flatten each half into a disk
about ½ inch thick. Wrap each half in plastic wrap and
refrigerate for at least 30 minutes.

4 To roll the dough, place a 12-inch square piece of waxed
paper or plastic wrap on a work surface. Place half of the
dough on it and roll the disk into a 12-inch circle. Dust the
dough's surface with a little flour, if needed, to prevent the
dough from sticking to your rolling pin.

5 Flip the waxed paper over, inverting the rolled dough
over the pie plate, then peel off the paper. Tuck the dough
into the pan, without stretching it.

Pies & Cakes

MAPLE SWEETS

144

6 IF YOU ARE MAKING A PIE SHELL: Trim the overhang to an even ½ inch, then tuck the overhang under, sculpting the edge into an upstanding ridge. Form a decorative edge, if desired, cover with plastic wrap, and freeze.

7 IF YOU ARE MAKING A DOUBLE-CRUST PIE: Do not trim the dough after you tuck it into the pie plate. Cover with plastic wrap, and refrigerate while you roll the top crust as in step 4.

8 Fill the pie, run a moistened fingertip around the rim of the bottom crust, and lay the top sheet of dough over the filling. Press down slightly where you've moistened the edge, to seal. Trim the overhang to an even ½ inch, then tuck it under, sculpting the edge into an upstanding ridge. Form a decorative edge, if desired, and poke three or four steam vents in the top crust with the tines of a fork. Bake as directed.

9 TO PARTIALLY PREBAKE A PIE SHELL: Preheat the oven to 425°F/220°C. Line the frozen shell with a 12-inch square of aluminum foil, tucking it into the contours of the pan. Spread about 2 cups of dried rice or beans in the bottom and slightly up the sides of the foil. Bake the crust in the lower part of the oven for 15 minutes, then carefully lift out the foil and beans. Prick the bottom several times with a fork, so steam can escape. Lower the oven temperature to 375°F/190°C and bake for another 10 minutes. Let cool on a wire rack.

10 TO FULLY PREBAKE A PIE SHELL: Proceed as above, but bake the crust for about 20 minutes after lowering the heat, until evenly browned.

Simple Rhubarb Pie

I WENT THROUGH ALL SORTS of convulsions trying to make this an "interesting" pie. I added strawberries, cherries, and on and on, because I was afraid rhubarb would live up to its reputation as something of a culinary wallflower. Each time, the pie was great, but the subtle rhubarb and maple flavors were being crowded out by my tampering. When I finally woke up and kept just rhubarb and maple, I knew I'd hit the mark. Chalk one up for simplicity.

Ingredients

- ½ recipe Flaky Butter Crust (page 144) or other pie dough
- 5 cups sliced rhubarb (½-inch pieces)
- ¼ cup sugar
- ⅔ cup pure maple syrup
- 1 teaspoon vanilla extract
- ¼ cup unbleached all-purpose flour
- Oat-Crumb Topping (page 165)

1 Prepare the pie shell according to the directions, line a 9-inch pie plate with the pastry, and refrigerate or freeze. Preheat the oven to 400°F/200°C.

2 Combine the rhubarb with the sugar in a bowl. Stir, then set aside for 15 minutes. Stir in the maple syrup, vanilla, and flour.

3 Turn the filling into the chilled pie shell and even out the top. Bake on the lower rack of the oven for 20 minutes.

4 Remove the pie from the oven, lower the oven temperature to 375°F/190°C, and place the pie on a baking sheet. Spread the topping evenly over the pie and return it to the oven, on the middle rack. Bake for another 40 to 50 minutes, until the juices bubble thickly. Let cool on a rack. Slice and serve when still slightly warm.

First you've got a clear liquid, and then it starts getting its color. And then it starts smelling like syrup.

— Mason Maddox, Colvin Run Mill

Upside-Down Skillet Pear Tart

THIS RUSTIC TART, baked in a cast-iron skillet, is sublime. This is just the tart to bring along to a fall potluck or party.

Ingredients

- ½ recipe Flaky Butter Crust (page 144) or other pie dough
- 2 tablespoons butter
- ⅓ cup pure maple syrup
- 2 tablespoons sugar
- 6 large pears, peeled, halved, and cored

---

1 Prepare the pastry according to the directions through step 3 on page 144, and refrigerate. Preheat the oven to 400°F/200°C.

2 Melt the butter in a medium cast-iron skillet. Stir in the maple syrup and sugar and bring to a low boil, stirring. Boil for 1½ minutes, then remove from the heat.

3 Arrange the pears in the skillet, rounded side down and points toward the center. Put two halves in the center, pointed in opposite directions. Any remaining halves can be sliced and interspersed on top of the others. Try to keep the top level of the pears even, but don't lose any sleep over it — it's bound to be jagged.

4 Roll the pastry into a 12-inch circle. Lay it on top of the pears and tuck the edge down between the pears and the side of the skillet. Make two or three wide slashes in the crust, so steam can escape. Bake for 45 minutes. Remove the tart from the oven and let cool for 10 minutes.

5 Place a plate directly on top of the crust. Ideally, it should just fit the skillet. Quickly invert the tart, tilting it slightly away from you to avoid getting hot syrup on your hands and arms. (This is best done over a sink.) Let cool for at least 15 minutes before cutting. It will probably be a little juicy; that's fine. Any juice can be spooned over the pears to glaze them.

Pies & Cakes

MAPLE SWEETS

Buttermilk-Maple Spice Cake

I LIKE TO MAKE simple cakes, such as this one, in general. The spices can be increased, but don't go too heavy on them or you'll mask the subtle maple flavor. A good snack item for brown baggers or for dessert, with whipped cream.

Ingredients

- 1 cup unbleached all-purpose flour
- ½ cup whole-wheat flour
- 1 teaspoon baking powder
- 1 teaspoon baking soda
- ½ teaspoon ground cinnamon
- ½ teaspoon ground ginger
- ½ teaspoon salt
- ¼ teaspoon ground cloves
- ¼ teaspoon ground nutmeg
- Pinch of cayenne pepper
- 2 eggs, lightly beaten
- ⅔ cup buttermilk
- ½ cup pure maple syrup
- ⅓ cup vegetable oil
- 1 tablespoon blackstrap molasses

1 Preheat the oven to 350°F/180°C. Grease a 9-inch square baking pan.

2 Sift the flours, baking powder, baking soda, cinnamon, ginger, salt, cloves, nutmeg, and cayenne into a large bowl. Set aside.

3 In a separate bowl, blend the eggs, buttermilk, maple syrup, oil, and molasses.

4 Make a well in the dry mixture and stir in the egg mixture, just until smooth; do not beat. Pour the batter into the prepared pan and bake for 30 minutes, or until a tester inserted into the center comes out clean. Let cool in the pan.

Pineapple Upside-Down Spice Cake

YIELD: 8 servings

THIS IS INCREDIBLY GOOD: pineapple slices paired with Buttermilk-Maple Spice Cake. I love the mapley good stuff that runs between the pineapple slices, especially near the edge, where it turns to goo/crunch. Instead of pineapple, you might want to try fresh apple rings, or peeled peach or pear halves, flat side down in the pan.

Ingredients

- 1 recipe Buttermilk-Maple Spice Cake (page 148), liquid and dry ingredients separated
- 7 canned pineapple slices (rings)
- 4 tablespoons butter
- ⅓ cup pure maple syrup
- ⅓ cup sugar
- Whipped cream, optional

1 Preheat the oven to 350°F/180°C. Prepare the cake recipe, but do not mix the wet and dry ingredients together yet.

2 Blot the pineapple slices dry.

3 Melt the butter in a medium cast-iron skillet. Stir in the maple syrup and bring to a boil. Boil for 1 minute, stir in the sugar, and boil for 1 minute longer. Remove from the heat and arrange the pineapple slices in the pan — one in the center and the remaining slices around it.

4 Make a well in the dry ingredients and add the liquids. Stir just until blended. Pour the cake batter over the pineapple slices.

5 Bake for 30 minutes, or until a tester inserted into the center comes out clean. Remove from the oven and let sit for 2 minutes. Put a plate on top of the cake and invert, rearranging the pineapple as necessary and scraping any juices from the pan over the cake. Serve hot or warm, with whipped cream, if desired.

Whole-Wheat Maple Sticky Cake

YIELD: 9–12 servings

AN **"EVERYDAY CAKE,"** this is long on wholesome goodness and short on fuss and bother. *Scrumptious* doesn't begin to do it justice. The icing on the cake, quite literally, is a maple–brown sugar mixture that's spooned on when the cake has cooled, then broiled to golden perfection. The topping turns crunchy at first, but then softens into a sticky, saturating coconut glaze.

Ingredients

- ¾ cup milk
- 3 tablespoons butter, cut into ½-inch pieces
- 3 large eggs, at room temperature
- 1⅓ cups sugar
- 1½ teaspoons vanilla extract
- ¾ cup unbleached all-purpose flour
- ¾ cup whole-wheat pastry flour (see Note)
- 2 teaspoons baking powder
- ½ teaspoon salt

Maple Sticky Glaze

- ½ cup packed brown sugar
- ⅓ cup pure maple syrup
- ¼ cup heavy cream
- 6 tablespoons butter
- ¾ cup sweetened or unsweetened flaked coconut

1 Preheat the oven to 350°F/180°C. Butter a 9-inch square baking pan.

2 Combine the milk and butter in a small saucepan. Heat gently, just until the butter melts. Set aside.

3 Combine the eggs and sugar in a large bowl and, using an electric mixer, beat on medium-high speed for about 3 minutes, or until light and airy. Blend in the vanilla.

4 Sift or sieve the flours, baking powder, and salt into another bowl. Add the dry ingredients to the beaten egg mixture, about one-third at a time, mixing on low speed after each addition. Add the milk mixture, half at a time, beating on low speed after each addition, just until smooth.

5 Pour the batter into the prepared pan. Bake on the center oven rack for 30 to 35 minutes, until the top feels springy to the touch and a tester inserted into the center comes out clean. Transfer to a rack and let cool for 30 to 60 minutes, then poke the top of the cake, several dozen times, with a toothpick (so the glaze can seep in).

6 FOR THE GLAZE: Turn on your oven's broiler. Combine the sugar, maple syrup, cream, butter, and coconut in a saucepan. Heat, stirring, just until it bubbles. Spoon the glaze evenly over the cake. Broil 5 to 6 inches from the heat for 2 to 4 minutes, until the topping is golden brown. Watch it carefully. Transfer the cake to a wire rack, then slice and serve when you're ready.

Note: Whole-wheat pastry flour is available in health food stores. It's a soft wheat flour that works well in cakes, muffins, and other quick breads where tenderness is desirable.

Pies & Cakes

MAPLE SWEETS

151

Tawny Maple Cheesecake

YIELD: 16 servings

I KNOW A THING OR TWO about cheesecakes, having spent a fair chunk of my youth cruising the New Jersey diner circuit. I know, for instance, that I like mine light, moist, and creamy — and hold the canned fruit toppings, please. That's why I like this one. This is wonderful with a cup of coffee, about an hour after dinner (or before breakfast).

Ingredients

- 1¼ cups fine graham cracker crumbs
- 5 tablespoons sugar
- 5 tablespoons butter, softened
- ¾ cup pure maple syrup
- ¼ cup heavy cream, cold
- 24 ounces (three 8-ounce packages) cream cheese, softened
- 3 eggs, at room temperature
- 1½ cups sour cream, at room temperature
- 1½ teaspoons vanilla extract

1 Combine the cracker crumbs and 1 tablespoon of the sugar in a small bowl with the softened butter. Combine thoroughly, then press into the bottom of a 9-inch springform pan. Place in the freezer. Preheat the oven to 350°F/180°C.

2 Bring the maple syrup to a boil in a medium saucepan over medium heat. Boil for 3 minutes, remove from the heat, and stir in the heavy cream. Scrape into a bowl and refrigerate.

3 Using a heavy-duty electric mixer, cream the cream cheese until light and fluffy. Add the remaining 4 tablespoons sugar and beat briefly, then add the eggs, one at a time, incorporating after each addition. When the maple syrup mixture is no longer warm to the touch, gradually beat it in, followed by the sour cream and vanilla.

4 Scrape into the chilled pan and bake for 1 hour. Carefully transfer to a wire rack and let cool thoroughly. Cover, then chill for at least 6 hours before serving.

[Maple syrup] is readily and economically produced, almost rivaling the snow in whiteness and purity, pleasant to the sight, and exceedingly pleasant to the taste.

— S. Scudder, in a letter to the editor of *American Agriculturist*, February 1858

Maggie Brox

MAGGIE BROX started sugaring in the mid-1970s. She and her then-husband put out some taps on borrowed land in Rumney, New Hampshire, collecting sap in a gathering tank attached to a dozer. Today she taps her own sugar bush at Butternut Farm, where people can stop by the sugarhouse in March and April and fill up their jars. I caught up with her when the 2001 syrup season was just winding down.

K: People have an idealized image of sugaring, like the scene on syrup cans: kids emptying sap buckets into gathering tanks on horse-drawn sleds, that sort of thing. Tell me a little about the reality.

M: Well, almost no one uses buckets anymore, except the hobbyists. Some producers hang a few buckets around the sugarhouse for show, but everyone uses tubing these days. Gravity carries the sap from the trees right to the sugarhouse.

K: Any problems with the tubing?

M: Oh, yeah. The moose walk right through it and tear it down. Squirrels and bears like to chew on it. So it has to be repaired periodically. And cleaned.

K: What misconceptions do people have about maple syrup?

M: They don't realize just how much sap it takes to make a gallon of syrup. Or that it's made from sap at all. They think it comes out of the tree as syrup and we just put it in cans. And I've had people tell me they thought all maple syrup came from Vermont.

K: After all these years, can you predict when the sap is going to run?

M: Not always. It's supposed to run when you have warm days and cold nights, but I've had days like that where I got nothing at all. And I've seen it run when it's 33°F and snowing like mad. I've decided sap pretty much runs when it pleases.

Carrot Cake

WHEN MY FRIENDS Mike and Nancy got married, I multiplied this recipe by about a zillion and made it into a multitiered wedding cake for two hundred guests. And they all liked it. I think this cake gets its special character and appeal from the maple, whole-wheat flour, and ground almonds.

Ingredients

- 4 eggs
- 1 cup pure maple syrup, at room temperature
- 1¼ cups vegetable oil
- ½ cup sour cream
- 1 tablespoon lemon juice
- 1 teaspoon vanilla extract
- 1 teaspoon almond extract
- 1 cup whole-wheat flour
- 1 cup unbleached all-purpose flour
- 1½ cups finely ground almonds (almost the consistency of almond meal; use a food processor)
- 1 tablespoon baking powder
- 1 teaspoon ground allspice
- 1 teaspoon ground cinnamon
- ½ teaspoon salt
- Finely grated zest of 1 orange
- 2 cups grated carrots (about ¾ pound)
- 1 cup raisins

Frosting

- 12 ounces cream cheese, softened
- ⅔ cup pure maple syrup, at room temperature
- 1 teaspoon vanilla extract
- 1 teaspoon finely grated lemon zest

1 Preheat the oven to 350°F/180°C. Grease a 9- by 13-inch baking pan.

2 Using an electric mixer, beat the eggs on high speed for 1 minute. Continue to beat, gradually adding the maple syrup, oil, sour cream, lemon juice, vanilla, and almond extract.

3 In a separate bowl, sift together the flours. Then stir in the almonds, baking powder, allspice, cinnamon, salt, and orange zest.

4 Make a well in the dry ingredients, then add the liquids all at once. Stir just until smooth, then fold in the carrots and raisins. Scrape into the prepared pan and bake for 35 to 40 minutes, until a tester inserted into the center comes out clean. Let cool in the pan on a wire rack.

5 FOR THE FROSTING: Beat the cream cheese with an electric mixer until soft and fluffy. Gradually add the maple syrup, vanilla, and lemon zest. Frost the cake when it has cooled.

Maple Butter Frosting

FOR A RICH FINISHING TOUCH for the Maple-Cranberry-Nut Coffee Cake (page 40) or Buttermilk-Maple Spice Cake (page 148), this easy recipe from Jo Burnett of Burnett's Maple Farm in Conway, Massachusetts, can't be beat.

Ingredients

- ½ cup (1 stick) butter, softened
- 3 cups confectioners' sugar
- 4–6 tablespoons pure maple syrup
- ¼ cup chopped walnuts or pecans

1 Using an electric mixer, thoroughly cream together the butter and confectioners' sugar, then gradually add the maple syrup until the frosting is light and spreadable.

2 Stir in the nuts.

Free from Adulteration

MARY,
As you are going to town
Please send or bring some syrup down,
Some Maple Syrup and 'twill be
Bottled and labeled you will see.

JOHN,
Now, Mary, you don't want that stuff,
Of glucose we have had enough,
So this is what we'd better do,
Send to Vermont and get it new,
There, you know, laws are made,
Whereby adulterations are staid,
And if you doubt the label's true,
Why, testing it will prove to you
That in this State one can be sure
That he will get it clear and pure —
The other States no fines impose,
Perhaps 'tis pure, the maker knows!

— Vermont Maple Sugar Makers'
Association, 1894

Maple-Mocha Pudding

YIELD: 4–5 servings

CLASSIC COMFORT FOOD, this, the sort of thing we all cherished as kids and now secretly yearn for since the onset of rampant mousse-ification. You get a rich maple flavor here, intensified by the coffee and cocoa — a winning team effort. I ladle this into small glass dessert bowls or goblets and serve with plenty of whipped cream.

Ingredients

- 3 tablespoons cornstarch
- 1 tablespoon instant espresso powder or instant coffee
- 1 teaspoon unsweetened cocoa powder
- Pinch of salt
- 3 egg yolks
- 3 cups milk
- ½ cup pure maple syrup
- 1 tablespoon butter, cut into pieces
- 1 teaspoon vanilla extract

1 Combine the cornstarch, instant espresso, cocoa powder, and salt in a large pot and whisk to mix. Whisk the egg yolks slightly in a medium bowl, then add the milk and maple syrup. Stir into the cornstarch mixture and begin to heat over medium-high heat.

2 Gradually bring the mixture to a boil, stirring gently but constantly. Be sure to scrape the sides as you stir. When the mixture finally comes to a boil, boil for 1 minute, stirring. Remove from the heat and stir in the butter and vanilla.

3 Ladle into four or five individual serving bowls. To prevent a skin from forming, place a piece of waxed paper, cut to size, on top of each. Let cool, then chill for several hours before serving.

Indian Pudding

YIELD: About 8 servings

INDIAN PUDDING IS THE OLDEST New England dessert on record, from what I understand. One taste of this soft, creamy maple version and you'll quickly understand why this dessert has a history behind it. A number of restaurants have built their reputations on their versions of Indian pudding, including the famous Durgin-Park in Boston. I've had theirs; this one's better. Serve with plenty of vanilla ice cream.

Ingredients

- 5 cups milk
- ⅔ cup cornmeal
- 1 cup pure maple syrup
- 1 cup raisins or finely chopped dried dates
- 4 tablespoons butter
- 1 tablespoon blackstrap molasses
- ½ teaspoon ground cinnamon
- ½ teaspoon ground ginger
- ½ teaspoon salt

1 Preheat the oven to 300°F/150°C. Grease a shallow, 9- by 13-inch casserole dish.

2 Heat the milk in a large pot over medium heat. Slowly sprinkle in the cornmeal, whisking as you do so. Switch to a wooden spoon and continue to cook and stir until the mixture has thickened, about 10 minutes. Decrease the heat, add the maple syrup, raisins, butter, molasses, cinnamon, ginger, and salt, and stir for another minute or two. Pour into the prepared baking dish and bake for 2½ hours. Serve warm.

Do not think that you know it all, for maple sugar making is a science about which you may learn something every season if you are observing.

— Advice from an 1894 booklet published by the Vermont Maple Sugar Makers' Association

Souffléd Pumpkin Bread Pudding

YIELD: 8 or more servings

HERE'S A SCRUMPTIOUS dessert with a split personality, part soufflé and part bread pudding, depending on when you choose to serve it. It comes out of the oven all puffy and dramatic and quite serve-able right away, but soon settles and takes on the compact texture more typical of a bread pudding. Personally, I like it best cold, the day after it's baked, served with a sauce of lightly sweetened sour cream or whipped cream and a drizzle of maple syrup.

Ingredients

- 4 eggs, separated
- 1 cup pumpkin purée
- 1 cup milk
- ½ cup heavy cream
- ½ cup pure maple syrup
- ⅓ cup granulated sugar
- 1 teaspoon vanilla extract
- ½ teaspoon ground cinnamon
- ½ teaspoon ground ginger
- ¼ teaspoon ground allspice
- ¼ teaspoon salt
- 5 cups day-old bread cubes (use leftover croissants, or French bread with the crusts removed)
- 2 tablespoons butter, cold, plus a little more, softened, for the pan
- ¼ cup firmly packed brown sugar

1 Whisk the egg yolks and pumpkin in a large bowl. Add the milk, cream, maple syrup, granulated sugar, vanilla, cinnamon, ginger, allspice, and salt. Whisk well, to blend, then add the bread cubes. Stir gently but thoroughly, until all the bread is well coated. Cover with plastic wrap and refrigerate for 1 hour, stirring once or twice.

2 Preheat the oven to 350°F/180°C. Get out a large shallow casserole dish. Get out a medium (2- to 2½-quart) casserole dish that will fit inside the first one. Butter the smaller casserole well.

3 Using an electric mixer, beat the egg whites in a clean dry bowl until they hold soft peaks. Add the beaten whites to the pudding mixture and fold them in gently. Transfer the pudding to the buttered casserole. Cut the 2 tablespoons cold butter into small pieces. Sprinkle the top with the butter pieces and the brown sugar.

4 Pour about ¾ inch hot water into the larger casserole. Place the smaller casserole in the water bath, then bake on the center oven rack for 50 to 55 minutes, until the pudding is puffy and crusted over. Transfer the pudding to a wire rack. Serve sooner or later, as desired.

Crème Brûlée

THE KING OF CUSTARDS, crème brûlée has probably done more recently to broaden the waistlines of restaurant-goers in the United States than any other dessert. This version, though slightly less rich than most, is taking its toll on my own midregion. Begin this the day before you plan to serve it.

Scalding

To scald milk or cream, heat it to just below the boiling point, until tiny bubbles form around the edge of the pot. It helps to rinse the pan first in cold water, for easier cleanup. Milk or cream can also be scalded in the microwave if you have a temperature probe; set it for 180°F/80°C.

Ingredients

- 6 egg yolks
- ½ cup pure maple syrup
- 2 cups light cream
- 1 cup heavy cream
- 1 teaspoon vanilla extract
- 6 tablespoons firmly packed brown sugar

1 Preheat the oven to 325°F/170°C. Bring about 4 cups of water to a boil and reserve.

2 Very *lightly* whisk the egg yolks and maple syrup together. Scald (see Scalding, left) the creams in a saucepan.

3 Gradually stir the hot cream into the egg yolk mixture, until blended. Do not beat it or the finished texture will be grainy. Stir in the vanilla. Ladle into six individual, oven-proof custard cups or ramekins of about ¾-cup capacity, filling almost to the rim.

4 Place the cups in a large shallow casserole dish, then carefully pour in the boiled water until it reaches about half-way up the sides of the cups. Take care not to splash water into the cups. Cover loosely with aluminum foil, then bake for 1 hour, or until a knife inserted near the center comes out clean. Let cool to room temperature, cover with plastic wrap, then refrigerate overnight.

5 About an hour before serving, remove the cups from the refrigerator. Sieve 1 tablespoon of brown sugar directly on top of each custard, spreading it evenly with a fork. Put the cups in a shallow casserole dish, then pour in enough ice water to come halfway up the sides of the cups. Turn on the broiler and broil the custard close to the heat until the brown sugar bubbles and darkens; watch carefully, or it will burn. Remove from the water bath and let cool.

Spiced Maple Pears

A DELICIOUS ALTERNATIVE to baked apples, these pears are as good for dessert as they are for breakfast. A member of Quebec's Citadelle Maple Syrup Producers' Cooperative contributed this recipe.

Ingredients

- 2 cinnamon sticks
- 6 ripe pears, peeled with stems in place
- 6 cloves
- 8 cardamom seeds, cracked
- 2 cups medium-sweet white wine
- ¾ cup pure maple syrup
- 2 tablespoons sugar

---

1 Preheat the oven to 400°F/200°C. Place the cinnamon sticks in a deep 2-quart casserole dish. Push a clove inside each pear and lay them on their sides in the dish. Scatter the cardamom seeds on top of the pears.

2 In a medium saucepan over low heat, gently cook the wine, maple syrup, and sugar until the sugar is dissolved. Pour the mixture over the pears, ensuring that they are half covered (add more wine or water, if necessary).

3 Cover the pears and poach for 45 to 60 minutes, until tender, basting occasionally. Remove the cloves, cardamom seeds, and cinnamon sticks. Let cool slightly before serving; they may also be served chilled or at room temperature.

Baked Custard

ONE OF THE SIMPLEST THINGS
in the world to make, baked custard
is a real crowd-pleaser when it is
made with maple syrup. One thing
to remember about custard is not
to beat it excessively, which only
makes the finished texture grainy.
Just stir everything together nice
and easy, then ladle into custard
cups. I think the maple flavor
comes out best when this is served
cold, but warm custard has its
proponents, too.

Ingredients

- 3 cups milk
- 4 eggs, lightly beaten
- ½ cup pure maple syrup
- 1 teaspoon vanilla extract
- ¼ teaspoon salt

---

1 Preheat the oven to 350°F/180°C. Bring about 4 cups of
water to a boil and reserve. Heat the milk in a saucepan just
to the boiling point.

2 With a whisk, gently blend the eggs, maple syrup,
vanilla, and salt in a large bowl. Slowly stir in the hot milk.
Ladle into six individual custard cups, filling each to within
¼ inch of the rim.

3 Place the cups in a large shallow casserole dish and carefully pour the boiled water into the pan until it comes about
halfway up the cups. Bake for about 50 minutes, or until a
knife inserted near the center comes out clean. Serve warm,
or cool to room temperature, cover, and chill.

Puddings & More

MAPLE SWEETS

164

Oat-Crumb Topping

A GOOD, GENERAL-PURPOSE crunchy topping for pies, bars, crumbles, crisps, and all those wonderful sweet things, this can be made with granulated or brown sugar. The disadvantage to the granulated sugar is that it tends to brown more quickly. But you can prevent excessive browning by loosely covering with aluminum foil.

Ingredients
- ½ cup unbleached all-purpose flour
- ½ cup granulated or firmly packed brown sugar
- ⅓ cup old-fashioned rolled oats
- Pinch of salt
- Pinch of ground cinnamon
- 4 tablespoons cold butter, cut into ¼-inch pieces

1 Toss the flour, sugar, oats, salt, and cinnamon (add more than a pinch, if you like) together in a large bowl.

2 Cut the butter into the flour mixture until the mixture is uniform and somewhat gravelly in texture. It shouldn't get to the point where it starts to clump together; stop if that happens. Refrigerate, covered, until you are ready to use. Freeze for longer storage.

Anything Fruit Crisp

This is a quick dessert to put together, especially if you've made a double batch of Oat-Crumb Topping and stashed some in the freezer. Simply slice fresh fruit, just about anything in season, to fill an 8-inch square pan. I'm partial to apples, pears, peaches, berries and rhubarb, or some creative combination of these, in my crisps.

Sprinkle the fruit with lemon juice or a touch of maple syrup, if desired, then spread the topping evenly over all. Bake at 350°F/180°C for 30 to 40 minutes, until bubbly.

Puddings & More

MAPLE SWEETS

Pear, Apple, and Fig Crisp

I LOVE TO USE A VARIETY of fruits in my fruit crisps, and I'm always on the lookout for new and surprising combinations; here's one that's particularly good and is a welcome departure from the usual apple crisp. If possible, try to polish this off the first day, while the topping is still nice and crisp; that shouldn't be a problem. If you can't, leave it at room temperature overnight and cover with a domed mesh food cover. (Aluminum foil and plastic wrap tend to trap moisture and soften the topping.) Vanilla ice cream is the perfect accompaniment.

Ingredients

Filling

- 4 cups peeled, cored, and sliced ripe pears
- 3 cups peeled, cored, and sliced cooking apples
- 1 cup diced dried figs
- ¼ cup pure maple syrup
- ¼ cup heavy cream
- 1½ teaspoons finely grated lemon zest
- 1 tablespoon lemon juice
- 2 tablespoons unbleached all-purpose flour
- ½ teaspoon ground ginger or 1½ tablespoons finely chopped crystallized ginger

Topping

- 1¼ cups unbleached all-purpose flour
- ¾ cup packed brown sugar
- ½ teaspoon ground cinnamon
- ¼ teaspoon salt
- ½ cup (1 stick) unsalted butter, cold, cut into ¼-inch pieces

1 Preheat the oven to 350°F/180°C. Butter a 9-inch square baking pan.

2 FOR THE FILLING: Combine the pears, apples, and figs in a large bowl. Add the maple syrup, cream, lemon zest, lemon juice, flour, and ginger, and mix well. Transfer the mixture to the buttered pan and spread it around evenly.

3 FOR THE TOPPING: Combine the flour, sugar, cinnamon, and salt in the bowl of a food processor. Pulse several times, to mix. Scatter the butter over the dry ingredients and replace the lid. Pulse again, repeatedly, until the mixture has a fine, sandy texture. Transfer the topping to a bowl and rub well, until you have clumpy, buttery crumbs.

4 Spread the topping evenly over the fruit. Press gently with your palm, to compact. Bake on the middle oven rack for 50 to 60 minutes, until the fruit is bubbling and the top is golden brown. Transfer to a rack and let cool for 10 to 15 minutes before serving.

MAPLE SWEETS   Puddings & More

166

Maple-Ginger Ice Cream

I CAN HARDLY EVER WAIT
until this is completely frozen to savor a spoonful — or two. It has a lovely gingery flavor that does not overwhelm the maple, and it does not require an ice cream maker. This is another recipe from the Citadelle Maple Syrup Producers' Cooperative in Canada. They sure know how to make it with maple up there.

Ingredients

- ¾ cup heavy cream
- 3 tablespoons pure maple syrup
- 1 cup light cream
- ½ cup milk
- ¼ cup confectioners' sugar
- 2 teaspoons vanilla extract
- 1 tablespoon peeled and grated fresh gingerroot or ¼ cup finely chopped crystallized ginger
- 2 teaspoons white rum, optional

1 Whisk the heavy cream and maple syrup in a bowl until stiff.

2 Heat the light cream, milk, sugar, and vanilla in a saucepan over low heat, stirring continuously until the sugar is dissolved, about 1 minute. Fold in the heavy cream mixture.

3 Pour into a 2-quart container, cover, and freeze for approximately 2 hours, or until mushy.

4 Turn into a chilled bowl, beat with a whisk, and add the gingerroot and rum, if desired.

5 Return the container to the freezer and freeze until firm, about 4 hours. Serve with maple syrup.

Maple-Walnut Ice Cream

THIS IS AN EXCELLENT, basic maple ice cream, good alone or with cake or pie. One thing I love to do with this is to create the Ultimate Death by Chocolate Waffles Experience. You put down a waffle (page 24), mound it with this ice cream, then scoop on lots of freshly sliced strawberries. Besides being a pretty special breakfast, it might replace the cake at your next birthday party.

Ingredients

- 2 cups light cream
- ⅔ cup pure maple syrup
- ⅓ cup sugar
- 2 teaspoons vanilla extract
- 1½ cups heavy cream
- ½ cup milk
- 1 cup chopped walnuts
- ½ teaspoon ground cinnamon, optional

1 Gently heat 1 cup of the light cream, the maple syrup, and the sugar in a saucepan, just until the sugar is dissolved. Remove from the heat and stir in the vanilla.

2 Pour into a shallow casserole dish and chill in the freezer until it is very cold. After it has thoroughly chilled, combine it with the remaining 1 cup light cream, the heavy cream, and the milk in the freezing canister of an ice cream maker. Process according to the manufacturer's directions.

3 When it reaches finished consistency, stir in the nuts and cinnamon, if desired. I like to let this firm up in the freezer for several hours, if possible, before serving it.

After being cooped up inside all winter, [I] still love to sit out under the stars at night listening to the crackling of the wood burning under the pan, and watching the flames lick the sides of the smokestack.

— Jeff Mitchell, sugarmaker

Puddings & More

MAPLE SWEETS

169

Iced Maple-Espresso Shake

YIELD: 2 servings
(or less, depending on your willpower)

IF YOU LOVE COFFEE and ice cream, this recipe alone may be grounds for remembering me in your will. It is simply addicting. On more than one hot summer's eve, I've been known to skip dinner in favor of a frosty mug of this. It couldn't be quicker to make — just buzz it all in the blender and serve. Refreshing!

Ingredients

- 3 ice cubes
- ¾ cup brewed espresso or other strong coffee, cold
- ½ cup milk
- ¼ cup pure maple syrup
- ½ pint good-quality vanilla ice cream
- 1 tablespoon coffee liqueur, optional

1 Chill two big glasses in the freezer. Put the ice cubes inside a folded kitchen towel and crush them, just a little, with a hammer.

2 Combine the crushed ice, espresso, milk, maple syrup, ice cream, and liqueur, if desired, in a blender. Process briefly, until smooth but with a slight slushy texture. Pour into the frosted mugs and serve immediately.

Beverage Booster

Maple aficionados often use good-quality light maple syrup in drinks recipes that call for simple syrup (or sugar syrup). It's easier than cooking the mixture of sugar and water needed for simple syrup. So think about maple in your coolers, daiquiris, sours, margaritas — and even lemonade.

Converting
Recipe Measurements
to Metric

Unless you have finely calibrated measuring equipment, conversions between U.S. and metric measurements will be somewhat inexact. It's important to convert the measurements for all of the ingredients in a recipe to maintain the same proportions as the original.

When the Measurement Given Is	Multiply It By	To Convert To
teaspoons	4.930	milliliters
tablespoons	14.790	milliliters
fluid ounces	29.570	milliliters
cups	236.590	milliliters
cups	0.236	liters
pints	473.180	milliliters
pints	0.473	liters
quarts	946.360	milliliters
quarts	0.946	liters
gallons	3.785	liters
ounces	28.350	grams
pounds	0.454	kilograms
inches	2.540	centimeters

Maple Producers & Organizations

For information about maple syrup production, local producers, or maple festivals, contact one of these organizations or your state or province's agriculture department.

Citadelle Maple Syrup Producers' Cooperative
819-362-3241
www.citadelle-camp.coop

Federation of Quebec Maple Syrup Producers
855-679-7021
www.siropderable.ca

Kortright Centre for Conservation
905-832-2289
www.kortright.org

Maine Maple Producers Association
207-793-8850
www.mainemapleproducers.com

Massachusetts Maple Producers Association
413-628-3912
www.massmaple.org

Michigan Maple Syrup Association
info@mi-maplesyrup.com
www.mi-maplesyrup.com

New York State Maple Producers Association
office@nysmaple.com
www.nysmaple.com

Ontario Maple Syrup Producers Association
866-566-2753
www.ontariomaple.com

Vermont Maple Sugar Makers Association
802-763-7435
http://vermontmaple.org

Wisconsin Maple Syrup Producer's Association
secretary@wismaple.org
http://wismaple.org

Mail-Order Sources

Many of the organizations listed above provide information about mail-order sources for maple products. The sources that follow offer specialty products used in recipes in this book.

Boyajian
Canton, Massachusetts
800-965-0665
www.boyajianinc.com
Maple vinegar and other infused vinegars and oils

Canadian Maple Delights
Citadelle Maple Syrup Producers' Cooperative
Plessisville, Quebec
819-362-3241
www.mapledelights.com
Maple vinegar and other maple products

Vermont Maple Sugar Makers Association
802-763-7435
http://vermontmaple.org
Their site features a search engine to find Vermont maple sugarmakers that sell maple sugar and other products online.

Wood's Cider Mill
Springfield, Vermont
802-263-5547
www.woodscidermill.com
Boiled cider, cider syrup, maple syrup

Acknowledgments

At the risk of forgetting someone (please forgive), particular thanks are owed to:
Richard Acheson of the Citadelle Maple Syrup Producers' Cooperative; sugarmakers Maggie Brox and Bill and Sue Clark; Angie Considine of the New England Agricultural Statistics Service; George L. Cook, maple specialist at the University of Vermont Extension Service; Jacquelin Coté of Agriculture and Agri-Food Canada; Wendy Heron of the Kortright Centre for Conservation; Bruce Martell of the Vermont Department of Agriculture; Tom McCrumm of the Massachusetts Maple Producers Association; and Kathleen Williams of Storey Publishing.

Recipe Credits

Recipe on page 114 printed by permission of Boyajian, Inc.

Recipe on page 155 courtesy of Jo Burnett, Burnett's Maple Farm, Conway, Massachusetts.

Recipes on pages 20, 65, 69, 112, 162, and 168 printed by permission of the Citadelle Maple Syrup Producers' Cooperative.

Recipe on page 125 courtesy of Bill and Sue Clark, Clark Farm, Wells, Vermont.

Recipe on page 103 reprinted from *Cooking in the Shaker Spirit* by James Haller and Jeffrey Paige, Yankee Books, 1990, printed by permission of James Haller and Jeffrey Paige, Three Hills Publishing, P.O. Box 110, South Berwick, Maine 03908.

Recipe on page 110 courtesy of the Kortright Centre for Conservation.

Recipes on pages 55 and 85 courtesy of the Maine Maple Producers Association.

Recipe on page 99 courtesy of Tom McCrumm and Judy Haupt.

Recipe on page 79 printed by permission of the Ontario Maple Syrup Producers Association.

Recipe on page 43 courtesy of Bill Schneider, Browning Brook Maple, Colrain, Massachusetts.

Recipes on pages 130 and 134 printed by permission of the Vermont Maple Sugar Makers Association.

Recipe on page 81 courtesy of Janice Wentworth, Warren Farm & Sugarhouse, North Brookfield, Massachusetts.

Index

Page numbers in *italic* indicate photos; numbers in **bold** indicate charts.

Other Storey Books You Will Enjoy

The Apple Cookbook
by Olwen Woodier

Apple pie is just the beginning! Discover the versatility of this iconic fruit with 125 delicious recipes for any meal, including Apple Frittata, Pork Chops with Apple Cream Sauce, Apple Pizza, Apple Butter, and many more.
240 pages. Paper. ISBN 978-1-61212-518-3.

The Fresh Honey Cookbook
by Laurey Masterton

Celebrate the flavors of honey with more than 80 seasonal recipes that focus on what's fresh each month. With different varieties of honey, such as sage or avocado, try recipes like Pork Tenderloin with Orange Blossom Honey-Mustard or Baked Acorn Squash.
208 pages. Paper. ISBN 978-1-61212-051-5.

How to Make Maple Syrup
by Alison and Steven Anderson

Whether you want to tap a single tree or set up a full tubing system, this concise, practical book will guide you through collecting, boiling, and bottling maple syrup.
128 pages. Paper. ISBN 978-1-61212-171-0.

Maple Sugar by Tim Herd

From sap to syrup! With full-color photography, readers can learn about and celebrate the history and science of maple sugaring, identifying and tapping maple trees, boiling and grading sap, and more, along with 24 indulgent recipes.
144 pages. Paper. ISBN 978-1-60342-735-7.

These and other books from Storey Publishing are available wherever quality books are sold or by calling 1-800-441-5700.
Visit us at *www.storey.com* or sign up for our newsletter at *www.storey.com/signup.*